EXCEL

MACROS

The Ultimate Beginner's Guide to Learn Excel Macros Step-by-Step

David A. Williams

TABLE OF CONTENTS

Introduction

Planning, organizing, estimating, and calculating to create better financial data used to be a tedious job that individuals had to perform manually. Many responsibilities, including bookkeeping, payroll creation, computation, etc. require calculative formats that need to be strictly accurate for productivity. Without a proper tool to help with these official responsibilities, a professional could not have survived.

Along came tools like Microsoft Excel, which have saved a lot of crucial time for professionals. Excel has been used for quite a while, and it surely has advanced to a level where it has become a necessity for all types of businesses. That is why learning it is important.

However, there is another side of Excel besides the usual calculative tools and tabular layouts that it is capable of. That side is known as Excel Macros. With an intention to educate the regular Excel users, this book will help readers understand about Macros. The purpose of this book is to help people get familiar with the world of macros.

Many are interested in Macros while going through Excel, but they feel scared to learn it because of the formula-based syntax it possesses, which feels like coding. If you want to learn Excel coding or have decided to try some projects that need the help of Macros, then this book is here to guide you.

Assuming that you do not have any knowledge about Microsoft Excel at all, we would like to first start with a couple of basic chapters to learn about this spreadsheet program in brief. Once that is complete, we will move on to the part where you will learn about basic Macros strategies, etc.

Note that, this book will cover Macros in later chapters with a vision to make you knowledgeable of its fundamentals in detail. It will also elaborate on the various uses, benefits, tips, and other basic aspects related to this coding side of Excel. However, you may have to go through other sources at later stages if you are willing to learn about its advance applications. For now, continue reading through the chapters one by one and learn about Microsoft Excel, Macros, and its fundamentals.

CHAPTER 1

•·+·————————•·+·◆·+·◆—————————+·•

Learning About Microsoft Excel

As mentioned earlier, MS Excel is a program designed for spreadsheets. This program is one of the most useful applications designed by Microsoft for its Windows operating system.

Since the day it has existed, it has been revamped and updated to provide you with tons of features, including macro coding, calculation, graphing tools, tables, pivot tables, etc. You get this tool as a sub-application of the bundle tool under the name Microsoft Office. You may already be aware of other MS Office applications like MS Word and MS PowerPoint. But, MS Excel is not the only spreadsheet program that developers created. Other programs that have spreadsheet features include Lotus 1, 2, and 3.

In MS Excel, you can see the layout designed with a grid comprising of cells, where you can use your keyboard to input data, such as texts, numbers, symbols, and other characters. The most common uses that Excel has are in scheduling, budgeting for home or office, accounting, and similar areas. Without it to help a professional, he or she would have taken loads of time to compute the data.

For people dealing with statistics, engineering, and finance, this application is a boon, as it helps them create histograms, charts, and reports, easily. Thus, its high usability has made it gain popularity as one of the most preferable applications on the globe. In some cases, people have been known to use Excel over MS PowerPoint or MS Word for their daily data creation, computation, and other features just because it is more versatile than the latter.

Basic Excel Operations

Now, this section will help you understand some of the basic operations that you can use in Excel. Maybe you are knowledgeable of them beforehand after using Excel beforehand. But, keeping in mind the various skills levels of the readers, this section will help you all refresh the features once again.

Furthermore, you will also learn about some shortcuts that you can use for basic operations in Excel in this section. Always remember that learning and applying shortcuts will improve your efficiency to complete your work on Excel sheets faster.

- **Creating A New Excel Workbook**

  To start using Excel, you need to first start by creating a workbook. A workbook in Excel usually has three sheets. For creating a new workbook, you can move to the File tab in the upper-left corner of your computer and click on the New button from the ribbon (ribbon will be discussed in later chapters). Alternatively, you can simply press the shortcut key combination: Ctrl + N to get started with a new workbook.

- **Opening An Existing Workbook**

  In some cases, you may want to view an existing workbook in Excel. For that, you can press the Open button from File tab. This will pop up a dialog box in which you can look for the file you want to open. You should be aware of the extensions Excel uses, which are: .XLS (for older Excel) and .XLSX (for newer

Excel versions). Alternatively, you have the shortcut key combination to open the dialog window using Ctrl + O keys.

A third technique is also there to open an Excel workbook. In this method, you can first open Excel normally, and then search for the file you want to open in your drive. Just drag and drop that file onto the opened Excel application. Excel will then open the file for you.

- **Saving A Workbook or File in Excel**

After you have added your data in the sheets of your workbook, you can use the Save option from the File tab in your application. When you are saving the file for the very first time, Excel will notify you with a dialog box where you can enter the name of your workbook. You also get to choose the location for your file. The shortcut key for saving the file is Ctrl + S. This will let you save the file.

Furthermore, if you have already saved the file once and named it, then pressing the save button or Control + S keys will just write the updated data on your existing saved file. This will not offer any kind of dialog box to rename the file. There is another shortcut key that you can use for saving your file instantly, which is F12.

To notify you that the file is being saved, you will see a loading bar flash on the bottom bar of the Excel application. Another way by which your computer notifies you of a save in progress is through an hourglass symbol.

- **Printing Spreadsheets in Excel**

  Often you require printing the created spreadsheets in Excel just like other Office applications. You can do that by using the Print option from the File tab menu. This will open up a window with the printing options for your sheet.

  The other way is through a shortcut key which is Control + P. The dialog box that opens can be used for selecting the number of copies you want to print for your workbook. The box will also let you choose the page range in your created sheet, which you want your printer to process.

  Note that the newer Excel versions do not pop up with a dialog box for the print button. Pressing the Print button takes you to another menu categorized under the File tab menu.

  Plus, if you want to view how the print will appear before printing it, you can do that by pressing the key combination: Ctrl + F2. Pressing this combination in a newer version of Excel will take you to the sub-menu for Print option, which has the preview of the print for your file.

- **Page Layout Feature In Excel**

  The newer versions of Excel also offer a feature where you can preview your page present inside the workspace region. This can be done using the Page Layout option. You can access this button through the View tab menu present on the top bar. Another alternative to view this Page Layout option is by clicking it from the right lower corner of your computer screen. You can find it right next to the slider for zooming your page.

- **Closing Workbooks and Excel**

After you have finished working on your workbook in Excel, you may feel like closing it with the complete application. Moreover, you may feel like closing the workbook that you have opened currently and switch it with a new one.

For closing a workbook that is open, you can visit the File tab menu, and press the Close button present in the options. The shortcut key that you can use for closing the file is Ctrl + W. Closing will cause the Excel to enter a state where several of its functions become dormant, as there is no sheet to operate. Note that if you have not saved your sheets, and have pressed the Close button, then Excel will notify you with a dialog box that informs you whether you want to save the file or close it without saving. Here you get the chance to save the file and name it or just cancel it without saving.

Once the workbook is closed, you can simply add a new workbook, open an existing one, or close the complete application by clicking on the cross button in the upper right corner. The shortcut key for closing Excel is Alt + F4. You can also use the taskbar of your computer to close the application by right clicking on it and selecting the Exit option.

CHAPTER 2

Using the Ribbon
And Other Common Functions

Now that you are familiar with the use of basic operations of Excel, it is time to move to the functions that are commonly used in Excel. Plus, this chapter will help you familiarize with Excel ribbon.

MS Excel has been classified into two categories:

1. The older versions that lack the ribbon

2. The newer versions that have the ribbon

So what is the Ribbon?

It is a layout that has been offered to the tool bar and the File tab menu bar. The older version of Excel and similar MS applications had a simple drop-drown menu with all the relevant functions. However, the newer versions have a list of options accessible through a dynamic layout, which modifies the toolbar content present below it or the body of the ribbon. This layout is quite simplistic and has been able to efficiently organize all the tools without taking too much space like the older versions.

Microsoft Office also lets you disable the ribbon look by pressing the Ctrl + F1 keys to hide it from the layout of your Excel application. Similarly, pressing the keys again will bring the ribbon back. If you do not want to use your mouse cursor to choose the various functions present in the ribbon, then you can use the Alt key combined with the highlighted alphabet in the ribbon as an alternative to navigating through the various tools (which can be done using the Tab key).

This can be done by pressing the Alt key, which will prompt Excel to offer you with tool tips next to each of the tool buttons and menu options. These tools tips have the various alphabets as mentioned earlier. Pressing the letter will take you to the section of the ribbon that you want to access.

For instance, if you want to use the Review section, then you can press the Alt key followed by the alphabet R, which is the alphabet assigned to the Review section. This will give you access to all the functions under the Review section display within the ribbon. After showing the Review section, the tool buttons will have the tooltips with them. As mentioned earlier, you can also navigate using the Tab key. Pressing it will highlight a button that is currently selected. Pressing Tab repeatedly will cycle through all the option in the ribbon for you to choose. You can press Enter at the highlighted option that you want to access.

- **Using Help In Excel**

  Times will come where you will feel confused about a function or an operation. Moreover, there will be situations where you may not recall the correct way of using a tool in Excel. When this happens, and you are not even online to take help from your search engine, then you may want to utilize Excel Help for aiding you. The Help option is accessible with the help F1 key on your keyboard.

Alternatively, you can use the Help option is by clicking it from the File tab menu. With the Help window, you will have access to all the basic operations and commands in Excel. You can also learn about advance features, steps and tips for troubleshooting, etc. All of these will make you more efficient and quicker while working in this application. Plus, using the Help window is easy as you can simply search for your query to highlight it in front of you on the screen.

- **Redo And Undo**

Just like in other MS Office applications, Excel too provides with the ability to redo and undo your input data. For using undo, you just need to press the key combination: Ctrl + Z. Furthermore, if you plan to redo your recent input, then you can just press the combination: Ctrl + Y.

Alternatively, the redo and undo functions can be performed directly by the Redo and Undo buttons present in the top left corner of Excel. Clicking either of these buttons will perform its relevant action. Moreover, these buttons will also let you see all the redo and undo actions you have performed in your workbook. This feature will offer you the ease of performing multiple redo and undo actions.

- **Copy, Cut, and Paste**

Another group of basic operations that are found on Excel, just like other MS Office applications, are the copy, cut, and paste functions. You can use the following shortcut keys to perform these functions:

Ctrl + C for Copy

Ctrl + X for Cut

Ctrl + V for Paste

Furthermore, you can access these from the context menu (accessible with the right click on your mouse). You can access it when you click on a specific cell on the sheet.

CHAPTER 3

Navigating Through Cells

Note that most of your time on Excel will be about editing and navigating cells. Using the help of just your mouse will not be a very time-efficient method of working on your project. To avoid consuming unnecessary time while working on this application, you will have to learn the shortcuts needed for navigating through cells.

Cell Navigation Fundamentals

With the help of the cursor keys, you can move around the Excel cells. As mentioned earlier, you can also use your mouse to click on cells, which you want to choose and edit. However, using a mouse will be a daunting task in cases where you have to deal with a large amount of data and multiple pages.

- **Navigating Quickly Through Sheets**

    As you keep inputting data on your sheet, you will have a considerable amount of data filled up on it. Unluckily, you will not be able to see all the cells on which you input or edit data, as the viewport has a limited view.

    Besides the use of the cursor keys to navigate around each cell on the sheet, you can also use the Page Down and Page Up buttons on your keyboard to view cells that are not visible in your viewport. These buttons, which are highlighted as PgDn and PgUp, can help you move down and up the screen at a much faster rate. This can be a much convenient way of working on the sheet if you get used to it.

Similarly, moving your cursor quickly towards the left can be done by pressing the Page Up button with the Alt button at the same time. And, for moving fast towards the right, you can press the Page Down button with the Alt button.

In specific situations, you can even use the End and Home buttons on your keyboard to move from the bottommost to the topmost cell of your sheet. Press the Alt button with either of the buttons will help you navigate to the extreme left or right cell in the currently highlighted row of your sheet.

You can also press the End button to bring the Excel into End mode, in which pressing the arrow key or cursor will take the user to the specific edge of the data region. This edge is highlighted with respect to the direction arrow key pressed.

- **Navigating Around The Edge of the Data Region**

In some situations, you will have to navigate your cursor to accurately reach the edge of a cluster of data. Note that this edge is not the end cell of the sheet, but the last cell containing the data input by you. For that, you can use the Ctrl combined with the cursor buttons.

For instance, think of a table of 4 x 4 that you have created with data filled in it. By pressing Ctrl + Down arrow key, you can move the cursor to the bottommost cell with data in it. Similarly, you can navigate around the created table by combining the Ctrl key and the any of the arrow keys.

As a reminder, the key combination explained above will work only on rows and columns that are fill with consistent data. If you find an empty cell between the input data, then the cursor will just navigate to the cell before the empty cell, and not cross over to the next cell with data.

- **Highlighting Multiple Cells**

  For highlighting many cells at the same time in your worksheet, you can use the left mouse button with the Ctrl key. For this, you need to hold the Ctrl button and then keep clicking the cells that you want to highlight together.

  A second method that can be used for this is by pressing the Shift key with the F8 button. When you press these buttons together, your application will enable the Multi-select mode. You will see it highlighted in the status bar and know that the mode is now enabled for you to apply it.

  You can see the words Add to Selection highlighted there when the correct key combinations are pressed. If you want to end this mode, then you can do it by pressing the Esc button on your keyboard.

- **Extension of Selected Cells**

  For selecting multiple cells in a column or row, you can use the Shift key combined with the relevant cursor button to move around and add the cells adjacent to it.

- **Selecting Cells Until The Edge Of The Data Area**

  You can also select the complete column or row containing data by pressing the combination Ctrl + Shift + any of the directional keys to highlight all the cells until the edge of the data region.

- **Selecting Cells Extending To The Next Screen**

  As you may have already seen, you are following a pattern when you are using an extension of selected cells. On combining the Shift key with the directional key, you are able to highlight multiple cells at once. If you just want to select random cells at once, then you will have to hold the Ctrl button and click the specific cells.

  Extending the selection to the next screen can be performed by pressing the Shift key with the Page Up or Page Down button. For going left or right side, you can press the Alt button with the combination discussed in the previous sentence.

- **Navigating Around Active Cells**

  If you have been editing a cell currently or have a highlighted cell and you want to navigate the cursor to the cell next to it, then you can do it with the help for the Shift, Tab, and Enter keys. Here is how it will work:

  1. Pressing Shift + Tab keys will navigate the cursor to the left cell.

  2. Pressing Tab key will let you move the cursor to the right cell.

  3. Pressing Shift + Enter keys will let you navigate the cursor to the cell on top.

  4. Pressing Enter will let you move the cursor to the cell at the bottom.

Another way of doing this navigation activity is by just selecting the F8 button. This will cause Excel to enter the Extended Selection mode. Entering this mode will let you navigate to extend the selected cells using the direction keys.

CHAPTER 4

Formatting Functions and Shortcuts

By now, you are familiar with the fundamentals of Excel. You will notice that your speed and efficiency while using this application has improved considerably. Your efficiency may have been further improved if you are using the shortcut key combinations subconsciously. This way, you can shorten the time you take to work on the sheets.

Text Formatting Fundamentals in Excel

After you have been able to master the combinations and navigation tools from the previous chapters, your next basic tutorial is to learn about the fundamentals of formatting text in Excel. Here are a couple of easy and common shortcut combinations for formatting text in this application.

1. To start with the formatting of a specific text, you can highlight the text or click on the particular cell that you want to be formatted. For making the text bold in a particular cell, you can press Ctrl + B keys.

2. To italicize the text, you can press the combination: Ctrl + I.

3. To underline the text in the cell, you can highlight the cell and pressing the combination: Ctrl + U.

16

4. If you want to use a strikethrough, you can press the combination: Ctrl + 5.

You can also cancel any of the formatting tools on your text by repeating the combination key once again. If you want the same formatting to be done on another cell, then just highlight that particular cell, and press F4 key on that cell. It will cause the cell to be formatted to the same style as you did for the previous cell.

Dialog Box For Formatting

There is also a dialog box that lets you get access to all the common formatting options at one place and that too quickly. This can be accessed by pressing the Ctrl + 1 keys, which will let you edit the cell for appropriate styling.

This dialog box for formatting will let you format the text, align it, change the style of font, alter the border of the cell, etc. If you just need to modify the font of the text in the cell, then you can do that by pressing the combination: Ctrl + Shift + F. Note that, this combination will also let you access the dialog box for formatting, but it will also automatically select the font tab.

You can alternatively use the Ribbon, which comprises of more styling and formatting options than the dialog box. Accessing options other than the common ones is much convenient to access from the Ribbon.

Adding or Editing a Comment In a Cell

At times you will be working with a colleague on a sheet or workbook. In such cases, you may need to comment or add notes to a particular cell or cells so that the other person can be notified of your comment. This is a significant method for the people who are not present to work on the same document at the same physical place. With its help, you have the benefit of tracking all the changes made to the sheet efficiently. You also have the ability to use comments as indicators that is important when the workbook comprises of a huge amount of data filled in hundreds of columns and rows.

In addition, comments will also act as reminders for you if you want them to notify you at later stages while going through the sheet.

You can add a comment with the key combination: Shift + F2. Pressing this combination will highlight a small yellow-colored box, which will stay active at the corner of the cell. This box can be used to leave any notes or comments. Moreover, you can also look at existing notes or comments, which you can edit as well.

After adding a comment to a particular cell, you will notice a red-colored arrow appearing on the top right corner of the cell border. To see the comment or note on that cell, you will have to hover your mouse's cursor on that cell. Also, if you want to see all the cells that have been commented on, then you can press the key combination Ctrl + Shift + O. This will cause all the cells with a comment to highlight.

Adding Time and Date to Cells

Another option that you can try out on cells is adding time and date. This means that you can set the current time and date to a specific cell. This can be done using the Ctrl + ; keys.

Cloning the Value In Cells

For duplicating or cloning the cell values, you will have to first highlight the existing cell with the value, and then press the keys Ctrl + Shift + '.

Adding Hyperlinks to Cells

Adding hyperlinks to text or cells can be done by pressing the combination: Ctrl + K. Upon doing that, you will see a dialog box appear on the screen for the hyperlink. You can add the URL that you want the cell to link to.

Setting For Text Alignment And Other Shortcut Keys Using Alt Button

To modify the alignment of the text for a cell, you can use several key combinations. For instance, to align the cell text in the center of the cell, you need to first hold the Alt key. After that, you have to press H, A, & C. This is just a simple shortcut that you are using for the options present in the Ribbon.

Technically, holding Alt and then pressing H, will highlight the Home tab on the Ribbon. After that, pressing A will toggle the toolbar's alignment options. And, pressing the C key will trigger the align center function. You can press the Alt key to review the assigned alphabets to the various functions on the Ribbon.

Similarly, you can use similar formatting functions, which you can locate on the Home tab or other tabs in Excel's Ribbon.

Working with Tables

Tables have a significant use in various workbooks and sheets. However, most users are not using tables in Excel to that much extent. For creating a table in your workbook, you can simply press the combination: Ctrl + T.

To navigate to a row on your created table, you can press Shift + Spacebar. Alternatively, you can navigate to a column by pressing the Ctrl + Spacebar. For selecting your complete table, you can press Ctrl + A together.

CHAPTER 5

Introduction To Macros

Before starting with Macros, it is advisable that you first go through the other basic functions, layout, and options of Excel. Figuring out the Excel formulae will help you be aware of Macros and its uses in a much more efficient way. Plus, it will be easier for you to learn the advanced stages of Macros when you decide to move to the next level in Excel.

Nevertheless, there is no rule stating that you cannot learn Macros without going through the basic functions of Excel.

So, What are Macros?

If there are multiple tasks to be carried out in MS Excel, and that too in repetition, then you will need the help of macros. Macros are considered to be a cluster of actions that you can execute as many times as you want.

Sometimes you need to repeat certain tasks and functions in Excel. For a couple of rows or columns, this may still be manageable. But, if you have multiple sheets on which you have to apply a repeated number of functions, this can be tedious.

With the help of a macro, you are automating the process. As a result, you are saving your time. So, a macro can be defined as an action or actions, which you can execute several times as you feel like. Upon creating a macro, you are technically recording the keystroke and mouse clicks. Once you have created a macro, you can format it later as per your needs and requirements. Its extension is referred to as .MAC.

Macros comprise of a code that will initialize your work automatically in an application. It will let you add customized improvements and features to help you in fulfilling a task at a faster rate. And, all you will need to execute it is a click of a button. For applications involving spreadsheets, macros are a robust tool.

Think of a situation where you have to develop a monthly report for an accounting assignment. You will need to edit the names of all the consumers with accounts that are overdue in yellow color. Plus, you are tasked with adding bold styling to all the text. With the help of a macro, you can apply all these styling functions instantly.

The usual macro processor used for various purposes is a universal purpose macro process that is not integrated or connected with a particular software or language type. Macro processors are codes that let you copy a specific set of text commands from one place to another to replace it and automate the process.

Several ways exist in which macros are executed in MS Excel. Furthermore, macros are the official coding language assigned to Excel. This coding language is known as VBA, which is the short form of Visual Basic for Applications. Note that VBA is not the same as Visual Basic. The latter language is a core programming language that is required to create various programs, which users use for various applications. Visual Basic lets you create files with the extension .exe and you can execute these files in the Windows OS.

On the other hand, VBA is a different type of coding language. It does not have the ability to create independent programs or applications. You will have to use the help of an MS Office application (which is not just limited to MS Excel). In other words, VBA is a small part of Visual Basic, as both languages have a similar approach but the former only runs in MS Office applications.

In addition, a macro can be considered a tool that offers permission to add various functions in reports, controls, and forms besides performing tasks automatically. For example, the OnClick feature of a button is linked with a macro to initiate a particular set of commands every time a user presses that button.

On considering Access, you can assume macros to be a fundamental coding language that you code by creating a group of actions to run. On the development of a macro, you are selecting that particular action from a dropdown list that appears. After that, you enter all the relevant fields to perform each action.

Furthermore, macros give you the authority to process controls, forms, and reports without the need for advanced coding like in Visual Basic. VBA applications just focus on a subclass of commands that you can use for creating macros in Excel and similar applications. This way, it becomes much easier to learn and use macros for people who find it hard to understand and learn VBA codes.

You can easily access VBA in Excel. This coding language is a 4th generation coding language. Consider each generation to be an evolved language with the solution to confusing and unrecognizable symbols. It is quite easy to understand 4GL (4th gen languages).

For instance, check this code out:

Selection.Font.Bold = True

Even if you are not familiar with coding, you will still be able to figure out what this code is capable of doing. It will help you bold your selection. It may feel a little weird on first glance, but you will get used to this format.

For your reference and comparison with a core programming language, here is a C++ program. Have a look at it and see how tough it is compared to VBA.

printf("%d:%0d\n",tmp->tm_hour,tmp->min);

This C++ code will print the time in hours and minutes.

Surely, it will be hard for a layman to understand what all these characters and symbols mean. So, be thankful that you do not have to deal with coding in this language to work on Excel.

Building a UserForm for Excel

One of the things that you can do using Visual Basic Editor is create a UserForm. What exactly is a UserForm? It is a custom dialog box that you can create to help you with certain purposes.

When you use a UserForm, you can enable a convenient interface in your sheet or document, allowing you to enter data in a more controllable manner. This makes the data easier to view and use, both for you and other users of the sheet.

How to Build the Form

Open Excel and then start the Visual Basic Editor. You can use the keyboard shortcut of ALT + F11; this shortcut is set by default unless you have modified it, in which case, you have to use the modified version of the shortcut. You will also need to use both the Properties Window and the Project Explorer. You can easily find these features in the View drop-down menu.

One of the things that you should remember before working on a UserForm is that you should try not to double-click on anything, unless you have been given specific instructions to do so. The reason for this is that double-clicking opens a code window. If you do double-click, then worry not. You do not have to close the sheet to restart everything! All you have to do is close the code window by clicking on the Close button. You can alternatively choose to switch back to the UserForm design window by using the appropriate keyboard shortcut (by default, it is always ALT + TAB).

Head over to the Project Explorer and ensure that you have selected the current sheet that you are working on as the workbook. Then head over to the Insert Menu and then select UserForm.

Once you do this, you will notice that a new blank UserForm pops up within the Visual Basic Editor.

You should also be able to see a Toolbox. However, if such a box does not appear, then all you have to do is go to the View menu and select the Toolbox option.

You may notice that the UserForm has a dotted border surrounding it. This border can be expanded. By doing this, you will be able to change the dimensions of the UserForm.

Remember that a single sheet could contain multiple UserForms. This is why it is vital that you give appropriate names for each of the UserForms for the purpose of identification.

Now you can get down to adding textboxes and labels into your UserForm.

To add a textbox, choose the TextBox button in the Toolbox and then click on any area of the form that you would like to add your text. You will be given resizing handles. These handles provide you with the ability to resize the TextBox as your see fit.

Now, you can add multiple controls into the TextBox. For the purpose of this example, let us go right ahead and use the below controls within the TextBox:

TextBox - Name: txtLastName

Label - Caption: Last Name:

CommandButton - Name: cmdOK, Caption: OK

TextBox - Name: txtDate

Label - Caption: Date:

Label - Caption: Amount:

CommandButton - Name: cmdClear, Caption: Clear

ComboBox - Name: cboDepartment

Label - Caption: Department:

TextBox - Name: txtAmount

CheckBox - Name: chkReceipt, Caption: Receipt?

CommandButton - Name: cmdCancel, Caption: Cancel

TextBox - Name: txtDescription, Height: 45, Width: 132, Scrollbars: 2-fmScrollbarsVertical

Label - Caption: Description:

Once you use the above commands, you should be able to see a window pop up that looks like a form.

It should have the First Name, Last Name, Department, Date, and the other commands you have entered above.

This is a simple UserForm that you can work with. You can always modify the above controls to fit your needs and create a form that works for you.

Finally, one of the things that people like to do while working with forms is to move from one section to another within the form using the TAB function. You can decide how the TAB function works. What this means is that using specific commands, you can decide what section will the TAB function take you to next.

In order to set a specific order for your TAB command, then all you have to do is go to the View menu. Next, go ahead and select the Tab Order option. A dialog box will now open up listing all the sections of the UserForm. The order of the list dictates the order in which the TAB function works.

For example, if the order says FirstName, LastName, and the Description, then you are going to start with the First Name. When you press TAB, you will be taken to the Last Name and then if you hit TAB again, you will end up in the Description section. If you would like to change the order (for example, if you would like to go to Description after the First Name), then simply use the Move Up or Move Down buttons provided in the dialog box. This will help you perform the TAB function in the way that you would like.

TAB function becomes useful when you have to fill up the UserForm in a particular order or if you would like to change the order in which you approach the form anytime during your activity.

CHAPTER 6

Working With Conditional Statements

Macro can be used commonly to refer to macro objects, especially the ones that a user can find in the navigation window under the Macro heading. But, the reality is that several macros exist within one macro object. That is why it is referred to as a macro group. A macro group is listed as an independent macro object on the navigation window, but it is still a cluster of macros. Nevertheless, you have the freedom of creating each macro separately as an independent object, but it is not really a necessity. This is because each macro, even the ones in a group, has its own unique name for identification.

Each macro has its own individual set of actions as well. In general you will require more than one argument to perform actions for macros. As mentioned above, each macro has its own name, which you can assign to it. You can even add a number of conditions to control its actions in the application. You will find a detailed explanation of such actions in later chapters.

Note that if the macro group just has one macro listed under it, then you may not need to add separate macro names. The name of the macro group or object can then be used for referring the macro listed under it. However, macro groups with multiple macros will require particular names for each macro. If the column with the Macro name is not visible to the macro builder, then you will have to press the button for Macro Names listed under show/hide group in the tab menu for Design. Keep reading for more information about executing macros of a macro object or group.

Note that macro expansions are shortened using their macro names. And, each macro name consists of a cluster of strings that are unique. Each of these names start with a unique symbol or letter, like $, #, or @. So, macro names can be created with various symbols or alphanumeric characters as well. Often, it is recommended that you start a macro name with @ if you are using Oracle. Albeit, it is essential to have unique names to identify macros in various applications, but the global and local macros names can still be the same. In the case being discussed here, the macros in the local directory will be offered priority.

For referring to or creating a local macro with application level of control, you should use dual names, like Sample.'@JPUM'. Note that parts of a macro name with special symbols, like @, will need to be added within quotation marks (you can use double or single).

Syntax

- For local macro, the syntax is usually in this format: name1.name2

- For global macro, the syntax just needs to be: name2

The application's name is referred by name1 and the macro's name is called name2.

Arguments

With arguments, macros are provided with a value to perform an action. These actions can be about operation of specific controls, displaying of strings in a message window, etc. Many of such arguments are crucial, while others are just optional for processing.

You can find arguments in the window for Action Arguments that is under the Macro Builder menu.

The 2007 version of MS Office Access had Arguments option as a new feature. It does not let you edit the argument actions, but only view them similar to the action. With its help, a user is able to understand the macro at a much easier level, as he or she will not have to select each action separately to view the respective arguments. If you want your Excel to show the arguments menu, then you need to press the show/hide button for Arguments from the Design tab menu.

Module

If we speak with a broad perspective, a module refers to a box that is meant for VBA code. In fact, a module is the area where the written code is stored in Excel. Think of it like a cargo ship or port, where you can find stacks of containers for shipment and storage of goods, etc. Just like the cargoes are there in the real world, modules are present in the virtual world – in the case of Excel, modules contain VBA codes created for macros.

You can access the list of modules available in your workbook that you presently used in the Project Explorer. The Project Explorer is the area of the Visual Basic Editor or VBE. You can use other types of modules besides the standard ones. But, note that the standard ones are called as modules only. Modules also comprise of procedures, which will now be discussed in the next definition.

Routines And Procedures

With a procedure, which is a component of computer coding, you can perform a particular task or action. Technically speaking, a procedure is a cluster of statements that are declared with a particular statement. This declaration is ended with the End command. Note that there VBA has two types of procedures. The

29

first one is a Sub procedure, which is used for performing actions in Excel. Plus, you can start a sub procedure with a declaration statement: "Sub."

The second procedure is a Function, which is meant for calculations and returning values for the output. You will learn more about it later.

Statement

These are instructions that are used for commanding Excel to perform various actions. Technically, you can differentiate statements in two categories. The first one is called a declaration statement, as you read in the previous section. It can be declared by the name and is utilized for declaring a variable or a constant. The second type of statement is the one that is executable. These are responsible for specifying the exact action needed to be taken by a statement.

Another type of statement exists, which is known as Assignment statement. This statement type is used for assigning a particular expression or value to a variable or constant.

Object

The previous functions discussed above are meant for performing tasks or actions. You may ask yourself, why are these tasks being performed? The answer to it is Object. You can understand this phenomenon more clearly when you compare VBA coding with the English language. This will help you understand the logic behind the macros and VBA. Thus, let us look at English grammar to learn about an object. As per English, an object refers to an entity on which an action is performed. You can find plenty of objects in everyday life that can set as examples, like a computer, a bike, a car, etc.

Even in VBA, the situation about objects is mostly the same. This is because VBA manages and operates on the objects. Over 100 object classes are present in VBA, and this language operates various actions over all of them. Some objects that VBA influences are cells, worksheets, workbooks, cell fonts, and cell ranges. The most common objects that you will find in VBA codes for macro creation are Selection and ActiveCell. With ActiveCell, the Excel is pointing at the currently active cell, and any relevant action is going to be carried upon it in the VBA code.

On the other hand, the Selection refers to the object that has been currently selected. In a nutshell, objects are defined by their classes. Now, let us learn about classes.

Classes

As it has been explained in the above paragraph, classes are meant to define several areas of objects, including procedures, events, variables, and properties. Based on the above paragraph, you can think of objects being examples of various classes, or you can even consider them being blueprints.

As an example to explain this, think of running a business that develops motorbikes. For manufacturing a motorbike, a blueprint is going to be needed. This drawing will be needed to keep track of the design and other technicalities related to the motorbike. This motorbike blueprint is there to characterize all the features of the bike being produced at your organization. You can consider such a blueprint to be similar to classes in VBA.

With the help of a blueprint, your company can produce as many motorbikes as they want and they will not be confused about the design, features, etc. These bikes are similar to objects in VBA. Classes in Excel macros is an advanced topic that can be learned as you keep practicing the basics of Excel. Their relationship with objects is significant for sure.

Collections

VBA uses this term to refer to a group of objects. If you consider this word at the basic level, then collections are quite similar to the real world collections you know of. It is simply several objects grouped together. Furthermore, this group of objects can also be a collection if it is accurately related to each other. Thus, collections have the task of managing and grouping multiple objects together. More specifically, the ones that are related to one another.

Object Relationship With One Another

MS explains that objects have a relation with each other, as they have similarities with each other. However, the primary reason for a relationship between objects is because of the container they clustered in together. You can also refer to it as a containment relationship that lets objects with similar features being clustered together.

Another relationship exists, which you can apply to classes. This relationship is a hierarchical one. It features as such when a class is a derivation of a basic-level class.

Property

Objects comprise of various characteristics, qualities, and features, which can all be useful for getting the description of an object. With VBA, you have the ability to modify and conclude the properties related to various objects. To explain it better, here is a real life example.

Consider a dog. What do you think its properties are? It can be the size of its ears, color of its eyes or hair, etc. Besides the properties provided for this particular dog (which is an object), it will also have certain methods of its own. Let's explain that in the next section.

Methods

To explain what methods are, let us think of an example linked to English once again. It was explained earlier that an object is something upon which an action is performed. That action being performed on the object is the Method. And, Excel is performing that method or action on the object. If you recall in English grammar, something that performs an action on an object is called a Verb. So, your verb in English grammar is similar to method in VBA. In addition, let us take the dog example to learn about the components of VBA.

It was mentioned before that dogs can have methods of their own. What are they? What do you think about walking a dog? That is a method or action being performed on the object (dog) to complete an operation.

The Appearance Of Methods And Properties In Excel

In a VBA program to create macros, Excel is there to perform all the instructions that are given to it. After writing a macro code, Excel executes it and completes the commands. In any code, you will face properties, objects, and methods all clustered systematically to perform the basic action of running a macro. You will instruct Excel to perform calculations, return values, fit text in cells, change colors, shapes, etc. All these operations that you will be performing are the methods.

Arrays and Variables

In Computer Science terminology, a variable represents a location for storing a value. This storage location is given a name as well. The value is located in the memory of the machine. In fact, variables can be considered as storage areas for assigned values. Think of them as envelopes. What is the purpose of an envelope?

33

An envelope can be used for storing a letter, which has information in it. You can place the letter with the information in an envelope. In the case of machine language, the letter of information is similar to the value of a variable. You can even add a name on the envelope to make it more specific, just like a variable. Now, consider an instance where you want to provide someone with information that has been placed inside the envelope. Now, you have two ways of providing the person with the information related to the envelope. Either you can explain the information to the person, who will then keep opening all the envelopes to match the information that you have described.

Or, you can mention the name present on the envelope, which will help the person to choose only the specific envelope with the name you described from a cluster of envelopes. That way, the person will not have to open each and every envelope to check the information. So, what do you think is the better way to get the information from the above two methods? Surely, it is the second one, as it will consume less time.

Here is an example to explain this better:

Assume that you have dog, and now you have to take care of its diet. Assume that your dog needs eggs in its diet every day. For that, you have hired five individuals who will be feeding your dog with eggs between 5 to 10 daily. For this dietary plan to work properly, you are going to set a few rules for the hired individuals. Each person needs to feed 1 or 2 eggs to the dog.

You also instruct them to report to you and let you know the exact number of eggs they fed to the dog yesterday. Think of a VBA application to create this dietary report for your dog. In a condition where any of the individuals did not follow the instruction, which is to feed 1 or 2 eggs to the dog, then your application will send you a notification for it.

Think of this macro to be named as Dog_Eggs_Diet, where you will have to list two types of variables for this code to work. Your first variable will reflect the quantity of eggs fed by each individual to the dog. You can name this variable as "dietEggs." Your second variable is there to help with the storing of the ID number of each individual. You can name this variable as "personIdentity." Now, what is the procedure of creating the variables?

For that, you will have to declare the variable in VB editor. Upon declaring a variable, you will provide it with a name and certain characteristics. You will also instruct your Excel application to provide with a space for storing values. You can declare a variable in VBA using the Dim statement. You can find more information related to declaration statement in other chapters or sections. For now, just think of the procedure to function in this way without being confused about it.

You have the ability to declare the variable at several levels. The location where the variable is declared will show you the time when this variable will be applicable. For example, you have the choice of declaring it above the module. This variable declared at the beginning of the module will stay in memory as long as it is open. Plus, you can use these variables in all the procedures that are relevant to the modules being used.

Besides, you also have the ability of creating variables with a limited access if you declare it within a procedure and not outside a module. Such variables are limited inside the procedure in which their declaration has been made. You will be defining various variable types that store varying types of data. This can be done using the term "As." A number of variables can be used, such as Range, Boolean, String, Long, etc.

As an example for the dog diet case, the declaration of variables will be done like this:

Dim personIdentity As Integer

Dim dietEggs As Range

Now, let's understand how these statements can help with determining the track of the fed eggs to the dog. You will also understand how the variables are being used for this purpose. Note that a variable with just one value is referred to as a Scalar variable. You can use such variables when you need to consider just one item. However, in a case where you have to deal with a cluster of items related to each other, this might be difficult to utilize. In those cases, we use arrays.

Consider arrays as a cluster of elements that have the same relationship and data type linked to each of them. You can consider this function to be the same as that of a variable, which is used for holding values. The only variation is that arrays are used for several values at the same time. On the other hand one variable, or scalar variable just provides with one value.

Upon utilizing an array, your reference is based on various elements provided to the arrays that use common names. However, they are individually identified using numbers that are known as subscripts or indexes. For example, if you have a cluster of 10 dogs, and you have numbered them from one to ten, then you can call them as Dog(1), Dog(2), Dog(3), etc., until you reach at Dog(10). Now, considering the example of the dog diet code, you will now familiarize with a condition.

Condition

With the help of a condition, you are evaluating whether a statement or expression is false or true. After determining whether the expression turned out to be false or true, Excel will take the action of running the program or stopping there. This execution is carried on the statements that follow.

You can consider a condition as a statement that need to be true for an action to take place. Consider your dog diet example for coming up with a condition to follow in the code. Note that the structure for the conditional statement is in the form of If...Then. Upon observation, you will notice that you second declaration statement mentioned previously can be input with an IF...Then command. To be more precise, this is how it can be used:

If any of the individuals fail to follow the rule of not feeding 1 or 2 eggs to the dog, then your macros should notify you with a reminder. Note that conditional statements are not limited to just Excel. You can witness their usage in other programming languages as well. Based on the evaluated result, the If...Then statement will instruct Excel to follow the necessary protocol.

You can choose several ways to create your conditional statement for executing your VBA code. To give you an example of the conditional statement, please refer to the below code:

If dietEggs.Value <1 Or dietEggs.Value >2 Then

MsgBox ("You need to feed 1 or 2 eggs to the dog every day")

End If

Let us understand this snippet of code provided above. The starting code provides with two conditions that Excel will evaluate to be false or true. The code line will instruct Excel to evaluate whether the value of the dietEggs is less than one or greater than two. Note that dietEggs is determining the number of eggs fed to the dog by an individual. This is the condition where Excel concludes whether the individual has followed the rule or not.

If Excel sees that the stored value is 1 or 2, then it will know that the condition is true and it will run the second statement. If neither of the conditions are true, then it will not run the statement. If you look at the second line, you will see that it is another instruction that this snippet is providing to Excel in case either of the conditions present in the first statement is not false. In this case, if the individual has not fed any eggs to the dog or has fed more than two eggs to it, then Excel will return the message that is present in the dialogue box as a reminder. With the third code line, the If…Then statement ends.

Now, you have been familiarized with the technique of creating the variables for storing the quantity of eggs that needs to be fed to the dog daily by each of the individuals. Plus, you have also learned how Excel reminds the individuals with the message letting them know to follow the dietary rule provided. To complete this code, you will need another part that is considered as a basic function in programming structures. The following part will be helpful in understanding how each individual will be asked about the quantity of eggs they fed to the dog.

Loops

These statements are present to help carry an operation multiple times. In short, a loop is a particular statement that lets Excel follow a cluster of instruction several times. Just like the conditional statement, loops can also be structured in multiple ways. However, for the dog diet example, you will be using the For loop statement. The For loop lets Excel know to run the various statements over and over for each of the components. The loop statement can be added above the conditional statement to execute it properly.

The line of code that will be used for this particular group is given in the following way:

For Each dietEggs In Range ("B4:B8")

You can see that this statement is written in such a way to make the loop execute. You can see the representation of the elements (eggs) being discussed here by the variable dietEggs. In particular, this variable is the Range variable object. The ending part of the code talks about the group in which these elements are located. In the above situation, it is referring to the cell range from B4 cell to the B8 cell. For these sets of cells, the loop repeats the set of instructions given to it. For each loop, the conditional statement If….Then that had been discussed before is applied to fulfill the purpose.

The purpose here is to return the message if the eggs are not fed as per the condition. The loop will make sure that each individual gets a message returned to him or her upon fulfilling of the condition, regardless of being true or false. After the conditional statement, you will have to add another statement to make the loop repeat itself. For that you will use:

personIdentity = personIdentity + 1

Adding this statement will instruct Excel to move to the next individual in line and repeat the set of instructions comprising of the conditional statement again. This type of code is quite simple and can be easily understood and written. However, you can even create more complicated codes that comprise of several statements and commands, such as ExitFor or ContinueFor. These commands can help to relocate the Excel's control to specific portions of a code. The ending statement of a For loop is given by:

Next dietEggs

This statement ends the loop and lets Excel know to go to the following element, which in the case above is dietEggs.

Thus, you have been familiarized with the various functions and statements needed to learn VBA macro coding. You may have noticed that many of the terms discussed above can be used interchangeably. You can notice how all such terms work together to create a code that has a purpose to be completed. If you master all these terms, you will definitely get better at Excel macro coding.

CHAPTER 7

VBA and Macros

To understand VBA better, you need to know the difference between macros and VBA.

Difference between VBA and Macros

Note that these two are not the same, even though they have a close connection to one another. In some cases, individuals have been known to use the two terms interchangeably as well.

As mentioned above, the Visual Basic Applications is a coding language comprising of commands specifically for MS Office applications like Access, Excel, Word, and PowerPoint. On the other hand, Macros is not a coding language. In reality, macros is a just a sequence of instructions that have a very specific purpose, which is to automate various tasks in applications like Excel.

In fact, a macro is a cluster of instructions that you want Excel to perform for achieving a particular operation. With VBA, you are creating macros and not using it directly to create operations.

For example, if you have read recipe instructions, then you can consider them similar to that found in Excel macros. The aspect that you need to compare between recipe instructions and macros instructions is that they both are instructing to perform a certain set of tasks. Achieving a particular goal through such commands is the primary goal of macros.

Although the language used for instructing for recipes is in proper English, VBA has its own equivalent for macros creation. Thus, macros and VBA have a connection, but their technicality is not the exact same. However, several terms can be used within the two interchangeably.

VBA vs. Macros: Why Learn Macros?

For a long time, macros have been in development. And, their existence has been as long as that of MS Office. With macros, there is an input of DB functions that are generalized by utilizing MS access functionalities that exist. For any problems, errors, or confusions while using macros, Microsoft provides us with the Help option to resolve them. Plus, there is the Erase option that helps with the generation of macros at an easy and accomplishable level while developing them.

Furthermore, the commands and operations of the database can be implemented for generating macros in the Macros pane. You can then convert these macros into VBA for MS Access. In a majority of cases, you will just be required to make a few small edits to make the program run. All the spacing, functionality, and syntax is added to the saved file, which comprises of the VBA code. This code is specifically linked to the application for which it is being recorded. And, the best aspect of this application is that even a beginner-level programmer can understand this code and create it for running various tasks. With this process, users who are learning macros, are also able to understand about VBA code implementation.

Note that creating and recording macros is much easier compared to learning VBA programming. This is true for applications that are not that comprehensive and are present for assignments at a global level.

But, the codes that are complex will not be easy to understand for applications at an advance level.

Macros are an essential tool for those who find VBA to be harder to learn. Some options in VBA may even appear confusing at first glance for some users. But, learning and understanding them will open up new possibilities to understand this coding language. It will also help users utilize Excel, Access, etc. at a diversified level.

Learning macros may not be as time consuming as other languages, but to shorten the burden, you can target specific applications that you have to or want to use for your ease. For the ones who feel macros are tedious and time consuming, you should develop and try VBA programming for strengthening your basics. By building and learning after understanding VBA, you are able to understand how programming works. That way, you will be able to utilize them in other applications as well.

Macros will be useful for a particular set of applications only. However, as this book is dedicated to Excel Macros, then you ought to learn this coding language for improving your skills and reducing unnecessary time while computing sheets.

A couple of features that macros are known for are:

- Generating forms for multiple purposes.

- Performing loops with conditional aspects.

- Providing professional designs based on forms with interface linked to DB functions.

- Processing of background data.

- Adding modules for handling errors to help the applications run efficiently.

- Combining Word and Excel features linked to the database.

Why Is VBA Macros Worth Learning For Excel?

With Excel Macros, you are able to save a considerable amount of time for processes related to Excel or other similar applications. This frequent help offered through macros may still have a limit to it. Plus, when you are having a recording tool to work with, in this case macros, you have a high chance of committing mistakes.

With the advantage of VBA, you have the ability to comprehend your codes with better efficiency. Using VBA knowledge, you will be able to let Excel know the exact operations for running a code. This gives you the privilege of accessing more functions and capabilities. Additionally, if your usage of Excel is frequent, then learning VBA can be a plus point for you.

As mentioned earlier, Visual Basics Application is a coding language, which can be utilized with a number of Microsoft applications. While VB or Visual Basic is a coding language, VBA focuses on a specific version. Even though Microsoft has curbed the implementation of VB, VBA has gained momentum in helping various MS applications function more efficiently. Fortunately, people with little knowledge of coding, or the ones who are at a beginner level in programming, can still learn VBA due to its simple layout and user-friendly interface.

Moreover, users will get pop-up notifications and suggestions to use various commands for working using automated operations. This greatly helps in making the script codes function better. But, one needs to understand that VBA does require practice before getting used to the language. So, if VBA is a little tougher to learn than normal macros, then why would you learn it? The reason is the ability to create better codes, which is possible with VBA macros.

Instead of just pushing buttons on the workbook sheets, and letting Excel record the mouse clicks, you will have the full freedom and knowledge of using Excel macros with all its relevant capabilities and functions. But, it is essential that you know the correct way of implementing them. After regular practice, and implementing the macro codes in your spreadsheets, you will witness a decrease in the time you spend on your workbook, etc.

Furthermore, you will notice that the output predictions are much easier to comprehend, as you will be instructing Excel to execute the code in the way you want without any unclear facts. When you have developed the relevant macro using your knowledge of VBA, you will have much ease in storing the data. In fact, you will also have the ability to share it with your colleagues if you want to.

In short, the reasons to learn VBA macros in Excel is:

1. It is a beginner-level coding language.

2. It has immense practicality. You can use it for MS Office applications, including Excel.

3. It will be a great addition to your Resume.

4. It will help you sort out daunting tasks while working on Excel.

You can find many other reasons too, but for now – these should be enough to get you started with Macros.

An Example of VBA Macro coded in Excel

The best way to understand macro would be through an example. So, why not we work on an example of VBA macros to explain it better. Consider a spreadsheet that comprises of names, sales figures and store numbers where the employees are working.

With the help of the macro, the added sales figures will be inserted with their corresponding names. If you like, then you can use an online source to access VBA dialog.

```
Sub StoreSales()


Dim Sum1 As Currency

Dim Sum2 As Currency

Dim Sum3 As Currency

Dim Sum4 As Currency


For Each Cell In Range("C2:C51")

Cell.Activate

If IsEmpty(Cell) Then Exit For

If ActiveCell.Offset(0, -1) = 1 Then

Sum1 = Sum1 + Cell.Value

ElseIf ActiveCell.Offset(0, -1) = 2 Then

Sum2 = Sum2 + Cell.Value

ElseIf ActiveCell.Offset(0, -1) = 3 Then

Sum3 = Sum3 + Cell.Value

ElseIf ActiveCell.Offset(0, -1) = 4 Then

Sum4 = Sum4 + Cell.Value

End If

Next Cell
```

Range("F2").Value = Sum1

Range("F3").Value = Sum2

Range("F4"").Value = Sum3

Range("F5").Value = Sum4

End Sub

While you may feel that this code is looking complicated, it can be segregated into parts that will then be easier for you to understand. Eventually, you will have a better grasp at the basics of VBA.

Declaring the Sub

You can notice that the module above has the syntax ""Sub.StoreSales()" at the beginning. It is the syntax to define that a new sub has been created, which is known as StoreSales. Similarly, other functions can also be defined. If you have to differentiate between a sub and a function then the basic one is that a sub cannot return a value, but a function can. This is much easier to understand if you understand basic knowledge about how programming languages are written.

Your knowledge of programming languages will also clarify that subs are simply various methods used for defining, operating, etc. without returning values. In the module above, there is no need of returning a value, so a sub has been used in it. Once the code ends, it is written "End Sub." This instructs Excel that the VBA macro written has now been finished.

Declaring Variables

In the starting line of the program in the module, you can see the word "Dim." This command under VBA macros is for declaring a variable. Thus, "Dim Sum1" is instructing Excel to create a new variable known as "Sum1." Furthermore, we want Excel to know the type of variable we are looking for. So, it is essential to choose the data type as well. Several types of data exist in VBA. Through a good online source, you can locate them all.

Our example discussed above talks about currencies, so the data type used for the example is related to Currency. For that the code "Dim Sum1 As Currency" commands Excel to develop a new variable for Currency, known as "Sum1." Every variable that has been defined, requires one statement with the term "As" to let Excel identify the type of variable or data.

Using A Loop To Start The Operation

As mentioned earlier, some knowledge of programming languages will help you easily understand loops. Nonetheless, just understand that loops are an integral part of programming languages. They help in simplifying complex codes and modules. To learn about them in depth, you can look for trustworthy online sources.

Several types of loops exist. For the above module, we are using the "For" loop. Here is how this loop type has been implemented in the code above.

For Each Cell In Range("C2:C51")

[rest of the code that follows]

Next Cell

This code is instructing Excel to use iteration for the various cells specified in the code. In the above case it is from 2nd to 51st cell of Column C. Furthermore, the example has also used the object Range, which is a particular type of object implemented with the VBA directory. Instead of specifying the action for all the cells, macros use Range to list all the cells within that range. From C2 to C51, the total number of cells this function applies to is 50.

In addition, the statement "For Each" lets Excel know that each of the cells will be applied with an operation. The statement "Next Cell" indicates that after applying a function on each cell, Excel needs to move on the next cell. With next cell, the system moves to the starting of the "For" loop. It keeps repeating the process, until all the cells within the range have been dealt with. Thus, the execution of the code goes on in a loop.

Another statement that you can find in the code is "If IsEmpty(Cell)" Then Exit For."

Many of you might be able to understand what its purpose is, as it is almost readable. For others who are confused about its function – once the cells are all finished, which means has reached a cell that does not have any values filled in it, then the loop will exit.

For your information, you can even use other loops for this code, like the "While" loop. In this case, the "While" loop would have been a better option to write this script. However, to teach you in a flow, the example used "For" loop to exit.

Using If Then Else Statement

In every code, a fundamental statement acts as the main function to execute a program. In the script above, the If-Then-Else statement is the key to this program's operation. You can find the sequence of steps listed for this below:

If ActiveCell.Offset(0,-1) = Then

　　Sum1 = Sum1 + Cell.Value

　　ElseIf ActiveCell.Offset(0, -1) = 2 Then

　　Sum2 = Sum2 + Cell.Value

　　ElseIf ActiveCell.Offset(0, -1) = 3 Then

　　Sum3 = Sum3 + Cell.Value

　　ElseIf ActiveCell.Offset(0, - 1) = 4 Then

　　Sum4 = Sum4 + Cell.Value

End If

If you were able to understand the operation of the example above just by reading the code, then it is a good thing. It may still be possible that the statement "ActiveCell.Offset" has confused you a little bit. This statement, for example "ActiveCell.Offset(0, -1)" instructs Excel to search for the cell that is located on the left side of the active cell. The minus 1 represents a similar direction pattern as you may have known to be used in graphs. This example is letting Excel know to work on the indicated column cell for the stored number. If there is "1" located in the cell, then the value needs to be added to the value in Sum1. If Excel finds out that the value stored in the cell is "2," then it will add it to the value in Sum2 cell. This process continues in this way.

Excel will compile the complete code in this particular order working on each of the statements. Once the conditional statement has been fulfilled, then Excel moves to the "Then" statement to follow the relevant instructions. If the condition is irrelevant, then Excel takes the compilation to the next statement indicated with

"ElseIf." Another case that can arise is where none of the statements were able to satisfy the condition. In that case, no action will be taken for the script.

In the program given above, the combined effort of loops and conditional statements have been helpful in fulfilling the operation for the macro. The offered loop instructs Excel to operate through each of the cells that has been chosen for fulfilling the conditions.

Writing Cell Values

The final part of the complete macro script above comprises of the results for the various conditional statements. The code for that is given below:

Range("F2").Value = Sum1

Range("F3").Value = Sum2

Range("F4").Value = Sum3

Range("F5").Value = Sum4

With the help of .Value followed by the sign for equals to, the program provides each of the cells with a value linked to its specific variable. That is how this program for the macro works. Lastly, the "End Sub" instructs Excel that the program has been completed for the Sub. That lets the application to end the VBA macro. After that, running the macro with the macro button lets you execute all the relevant additions of the sales figures in their respective columns.

Various Building Blocks Used In VBA Excel

As mentioned earlier, a complicated VBA macros can be simplified if you break it down into various parts. You will find it much more logical and easier to comprehend in small sections. Plus, once you become used to reading and writing these scripts, your subconscious mind will understand the various syntaxes for VBA macro right away!

Increase your knowledge in the vocabulary of syntaxes, codes, and statements will increase your speed in typing such macro at a much faster rate. It will also improve your logic behind the way they have to be created, resulting in better accuracy of output. Plus, it will be a much better alternative to use macros than recording clicks for creating macros.

Searching online sources for answers on various confusing parts will give you a supportive explanation of such terms and statements in detail. If you are interested in learning about these scripts in depth, then you can even Google about them. Moving to an intermediate or advance level in macros will let you perform advance-level tasks, such as looking at your PC's information, emailing through Excel, and exporting tasks in Outlook.

CHAPTER 8

Locating Macros In Excel

Before proceeding with how to use macros, it is first necessary that you understand where to find it in your Excel program. You will first have to enable it in Excel. By default, macros are always turned off. So, you will have to activate it manually.

Here is how it can be done:

1. Open Excel.

2. Click on the File tab.

3. Press the Customize Ribbon button present in the box on the left.

4. Then look for the box near the Developer section, in the extreme right in the window.

5. Press OK button to enable the Develop tab in Excel above the Ribbon.

A Tip: When you are present in the window for Customizing Ribbon, you can also remove or add items from the Excel ribbon. If you have commands that you use quite frequently, then you can add those to the Ribbon to access them quickly.

Recording and Creating Macros

To start with macros, you should first create one. Recording macros is considered the simplest way of creating macros.

Here is how it works:

Pressing the record button will prompt Excel to literally record all the future activity of button clicks you perform. Once you have completed the action, you can click on the replay button, which will cause Excel to repeat the set of clicks it recorded for you.

To be honest, you cannot find a simpler way to understand how to create macros than this in Excel. Once you have recorded a macro, you can have a look at the recorded buttons to see if you did not miss something out. If you did something wrong, then you can modify your recording, delete or add functions and combinations, and replay it to check. Note that with practice, you will be able to understand the correct way it works for you. This is just one of the ways you can learn to use macros.

But, there are several functions that are not recordable. This is a significant limitation that macros have. Recording macros is an initial step that will help you get used to the tool, but if you want to devise a more sophisticated function, then recording your steps may not be a suitable method.

For now, you need to understand this simple and useful technique to record a macro.

Ensure that you have enabled the Developer tab in your application before you start. If it is not turned on, then you can go through the previous part of this chapter to learn the steps to initiate it.

Once you have enabled the Developer tab, move on to the following steps.

1. Open a new workbook in your Excel.

2. At the bottom corner on the left, you will find an icon near the word "Ready. " Press that button to start recording the macro. The icon will change to a small square, which means that the macros is currently recording.

3. Pressing that button will open up a Record Macro window. This window has various fields to input the name, location (to store the macro in), and a shortcut key input for the macro you are recording. Either you can change the fields or leave it to default values as it is. For this example, let us leave it as default. Press OK.

4. Press the A1 cell.

5. Type the text Salesperson and press Enter

6. After that, press A2 cell and type John. Press Enter.

7. Pressing enter will take you to A3 cell, where you can type the next name say Jeremy. Press Enter again. If you made some mistake, just fix it as you usually would do and continue with the next step.

8. Once you have recorded it, you can stop the recording by pressing the square button.

Now, it is time to view your created macro.

9. Press the Developer Tab.

10. Press the first button, which says "Visual Basic." This will prompt you with a new window. This window is known as the VBA editor in Excel. Depending upon your respective settings, you may see a varying window layouts, but the options should be the same, nonetheless.

In some cases the macro may not be showing in the window, but it is right there. You just need to display it there. Before learning how to display it, let us first understand the various options on this window. The box on the upper left is known as the Project window. You will be able to notice all the worksheets of your workbook, with the modules (macros are stored in modules) that have been created.

The window on the left at the bottom is called Properties. This window displays all the properties of the object that you select in the Project window. For instance, if you select Sheet1 from the Project box, then you will be able to see its properties in the Properties window. The box on the right, which is gray in color, is the window where your macro code will be displayed.

11. Expand the modules from the Project box.

12. This will highlight the Module 1. Double click it using your mouse to show the macro on the code window.

You should be able to see the following Macro code as given below, if you followed the steps accurately.

Sub Macro1()

'

' Macro1 Macro

Range("A1").Select

ActiveCell.FormulaR1C1 = "Salesperson"

Range("A2").Select

ActiveCell.FormulaR1C1 = "John"

Range("A3").Select

ActiveCell.FormulaR1C1 = "Jeremy"

End Sub

As per the previous information that you have been provided, you will notice that Excel chooses a cell with the help of Select method. After that, it records the value after the "=" sign for the property: FormulaR1C1. Whenever you need to input text in a particular cell, you will have to always add it within quotation marks.

The created macro will execute each code from the starting to the ending running each line that is missing a quote as the initial character.

CHAPTER 9

Locating Created Macro Codes

If you keep track of the time you spend on Excel while performing small, repetitive, and unimportant tasks, then you will understand how boring and irritating it can be. You may notice that filling up various cells in your spreadsheet, inserting, or formatting the text will take a considerable amount of time. You may a have the habit of performing these repetitive activities, and you may think that you have become quite fast in completing the task. But, it can be annoying to do so.

Think of a task where you just have to spend 5 to 10 minutes filling out every sheet with the same details about your workbook project and then sending it to clients and counterparts. Each sheet will take so much of your time just for this repetition.

In most of the cases, you are going to not yield any productive results out of this activity. In fact, this situation in Excel is considered to be a major example in unproductive and repetitive approach. While going through this book, you must feel the importance and power of macros to help you get over such repetitions. With their help, you will be free from typing and filling everything again and again.

Thus, you chose this guide and now, it will help you with performing the tasks and learning the basics of macros. Creating macros will now be discussed within this chapter.

You have been introduced to setting up macros in one of the previous chapters. Now, it is time to learn how to find them.

Location of Macro Code

As mentioned earlier, the Project Window will help in navigating various modules, functions, etc. On expanding VBA Project window, you will see two folders: one is related to Modules, and the other is for Objects in Excel. You can find various elements provided to you in the Objects folder. But, the elements will not be present in the Modules folder. Click on the plus sign next to the Modules folder to check its contents.

The components that are present in the Objects folder may feel familiar to you, but you may still feel a little confused about a Module folder and its components. In simple words, you can consider a module to be a folder for VBA program. All the codes that are written in VBA are stored in the Module folder. Upon recording a macro, you will find that its code gets stored in the module folder under the name Module1.

To view this VBA code, you just have to right click the Module1 component or double click it to view the recorded macro code. This will display the VBE macro code in the coding window present next to it. When you look at the displayed code, do you feel it is making any sense? Some parts that are mostly in English will make sense to you. However, other parts may still feel confusing to you. Another query that may come to your mind while going through the code is that why such instances such as changing the color of fonts, fitting columns automatically, changing color of cells, writing text, etc. requires such complicated programming? This question is a common one that many non-programmers have in their minds. The following section will help you understand the reason for that.

Implementing Excel Macro Code For Learning VBA From The Fundamental Level

A positive sign that you can agree to while learning macro code is that it somewhat resembles the English language. To make it easier for users to code in VBA, the use of structured English is relevant, which is quite similar to the common English we speak. The use of English words structured for certain operations is a key strategy that helps in understanding the instructions in an efficient way. This way, not only Excel, but the user who is typing the code is able to understand what the command is meant to perform in VBA. Understanding some words and instructions will also help keep track of what the program is meant to do at a complex level.

That does not mean that all programming languages are comprising of English words that make sense for the user. Some languages have specific syntaxes that are not easy to understand despite being in English. VBA, on the other hand, still is an easier coding language that gives a fundamental knowledge of how programming languages work for beginners.

Here is a small example of VBA code:

Sub Easy_Excel_Tutorial()

'

' Easy _Excel_Tutorial Macro

' Types "This is an easy Excel tutorial". Auto-fits column. Cell color red. Font color blue.

'

```
' Keyboard Shortcut: Ctrl+Shift+B

'

    ActiveCell.Select

    ActiveCell.FormulaR1C1 = "This is an easy Excel tutorial"

    Selection.Columns.Autofit

    With Selection.Interior

        .Pattern = xlSolid

        .PatternColorIndex = xlAutomatic

        .Color = 255

        .TintAndShade = 0

        .PatternTintAndShade = 0

    End With

    With Selection.Font

        .Color = -4165632

        .TintAndShade = 0

    End With

End Sub
```

After going through the above code, you may want to understand certain terms used in it that may or may not be confusing.

ActiveCell.Select:

This command is meant to point out to the cells that are actively selected in your worksheet. Any beginner will be able to fathom the use of the word "Select" in Excel or VBA. You can understand that this word represents choosing a particular selection. In this case, we are choosing an active cell.

Selection.Columns.Autofit:

Another simple command that has a clear purpose of selecting the columns and fitting them automatically based on their width. Any text that has been typed in the cells of this column will be symmetrically adjusted for creating a more prominent and good-looking column in the worksheet. The text typed in the cell will be completely visible and adjusted within it.

Note that such terms and commands will be frequently dealt with while you learn macro code. So, you need to understand its fundamentals.

The Fundamentals oF Excel Macro Code

To understand it better, we will now go through the complete code example given above. You need to examine it line by line to learn how Excel runs the macro. Even if you are not able to understand some or all of the lines in the program, you do not have to worry for now. The objective here is to help you understand the basics of the VBA macro code and its operations. Plus, it will show how Excel will follow the instructions step by step to change the color of the font, color of the active cell, and write the line instructed in the program.

Another thing that you will notice in the created macro is that the code incorporates various actions that you did not actively carry out. Do not worry about the lines that may appear useless at that instance, as the actions given to Excel will be translated into code eventually for it to process.

For now, let us understand the various parts of the programming code written:

1. Sub Easy_Excel_Tutorial()

The expression Sub present in this line of code is the short form for Sub Procedure. It is a type of procedure that you can utilize for developing codes in Excel macros. There are two types of procedures, and this is one of them. With sub procedures, you are instructing Excel to carry actions or activities within it. Besides Sub, the other procedure is Function. As mentioned in one of the previous chapters, the Function is helpful in returning a value or performing calculations.

Thus, with the code above, you are instructing Excel to create a Sub. To create such type of a procedure, you always have to start with the word Sub, after which the name of the procedure is added, followed by parentheses. At the end, the sub needs to be completed using the command "End Sub."

2. The lines followed by an apostrophe

You can see the lines that are given followed by an apostrophe ('). These refer to as comments and have the following features:

- You indicate comments using the apostrophe, so they start after the symbol (').

- Any line that follows this symbol is ignored by VBA until the end. While executing the code, such lines will not be compiled by Excel.

- Based on the previous action, the primary reason for comments in a code is to help the user get some information

63

relevant to the macro code. This way, it is easier to understand what the code is about. With comments, developers share information among themselves to clear the purpose of a particular code. Moreover, any recent modifications that have been made in the code are also referenced using comments. Almost all programming languages have their own ways of highlighting comments in codes to explain procedures better.

3. ActiveCell.Select

Just like the first line of code explained before, this one also selects an active cell in Excel. To be more precise:

- The current cell active in the sheet's active window is the ActiveCell.

- With select, the object becomes active on the current worksheet. The ActiveCell is the cell that is currently active in this one.

4. ActiveCell.FormulaR1C1 = "This is an easy Excel tutorial"

This statement is instructing Excel to write the line in the currently active cell. Let us check the various parts of this line one by one. By now, you have already understood the reason for ActiveCell to be there in the line. The part written as "FormulaR1C1" is there to instruct Excel for setting up a formula for the object. For the code above, the formula will be set up for the active cell.

The code R1C1 is indicating a relative cell, instead of an absolute cell. You will find more details about R1C1 later. Understand that recording a macros in this case is a relative one, which can have a varying active cell, instead of a fixed one. The formula to which this code is referring to in this case is the text "This is an easy Excel tutorial." This case wants the text to be filled in the currently active cell or the object.

5. Selection.Columns.AutoFit

As explained earlier, the columns will be auto-fitted using this command in the active cell. This will fit the complete text in the cell with the help of the command. The purpose of the various parts used in this command will now be explained:

- Selection: This is referring to the present selection. In the current case, it is referring to the active cell.

- Columns: This is referring to the columns selected using the command. In this case, the column with the active cell is bring referred here.

- AutoFit: You can understand the purpose of this word easily. The command automatically adjusts the width of the column selected with the active cell. Autofit is not just limited to columns, but also to rows. So a relevant code with rows in selection can also be used for serving the macro code purpose.

6. The Code From With ... to End With

Until now, the macro code statements discussed above are performing the two functions that it had been programmed to do, which are: filling the text "This is an easy Excel Tutorial" in the active cell, and auto-fitting it in the active cell of the column. Now, the code that starts with "With" instructs Excel to perform the next set of instructions.

These comprise of changing the color of the active cell to red. It may feel that changing the color of an active cell is a simple step, but in as per the programming limitations, this is a multi-step procedure to perform. To perform this coloring operation, you will have to use the statement With…End With.

The primary objective of this statement is to create a simple syntax for running a particular set of instructions for the same object at every instance. For this particular code, the object being referred to is the active cell. You can see in the main code above that there are two With – End With command statements, which are both serving their respective purposes.

These statements comprise of the structure below:

The code needs to start with the syntax referring to the objectExpression. So it becomes "With objectExpression." For now, you do not need to understand much about the term objectExpression. Think of it as a typename variable that is replaced with selection. In this case, "Selection.Interior" is the objectExpression for the first statement for With-End With.

Similarly, "Selection.Font" is the objectExpression for the next statement. These code or set of codes are mentioned in the created macro so that Excel can execute it by referring to the selected object. With the help of the "With" statement, you are instructing Excel to follow the necessary protocol. Later, the code is ended with the "End With" statement.

From the code you can understand the part within the first With…End With syntax. For your understanding, here is the code being referred to once again:

With Selection.Interior

    .Pattern = xlSolid

    .PatternColorIndex = xlAutomatic

    .Color = 255

.TintAndShade = 0

.PatternTintAndShade = 0

End With

Based on the above code, we will now explain each of these line one after the other.

- **The First Line:** This line is instructing Excel to refer to the active cell's interior while running the various statements. These statements are within the With-End With statement. To perform this action, a user needs to start with the "With" command, like done in the code above. This code commands Excel that the lines of code that follow after the With syntax need to be executed.

  The Selection in "Selection.Interior" refers to selecting the active cell, as explained previously. The term Interior here refers to the object's interior. In this case is the active cell's interior. As mentioned earlier, "Selection.Interior" together are referred to as an objectExpression.

- **The Second Line (Pattern = xlSolid):** This line is the first one after the starting of the With-End With command. It has been added in reference to the interior of the currently active cell. With it, the code is setting a color pattern for the interior of the active cell so that it does not choose solid colors. You can accomplish this by this:

  1. "Pattern" will help in setting up the pattern inside the cell.

  2. "xlSolid" will help in marking so that the pattern is solid color.

67

- **The Third Line (PatternColorIndex = xlAutomatic):** With this command line, you are adding an automatic pattern for the active cell's inner portion. This is how the parts function:

    1. "PatternColorIndex" will help in setting the inner pattern's color.

    2. "xlAutomatic" is used for ensuring that the color is selected automatically.

- **The Fourth Line (.Color = 25):** With this statement, you are instructing Excel to select the color that is needed for filling up the inner part of the active cell. The term "Color" is there for assigning the color for the cell. Since the number 25 has been added beforehand, so this makes the choice absolute, which in this case is the color red.

- **The Fifth Line (.TintAndShade = 0):** With this line of code, you are instructing Excel to choose a color that is neither too light nor dark for filling the interior of the active cell. The command ".TintAndShade" is being used for making a decision for the color to lighten or darken it appropriately for the active cell. In this case, the value for this command has been set as zero, which sets a neutral color for the cell. So, there is no lightening or darkening in the chosen cell.

- **The Sixth Line (.PatternTintAndShade = 0):** Just like before, this command is also set for choosing the color for the pattern in the interior of the active cell. Being set to zero, the pattern color chosen will not be a shade or tint for the interiors of the active cell. With the ".PatternTintAndShade" command, the decision for the shade and tint pattern will be made for the selected cell.

- **The Seventh Line (End With):** As discussed before, this line will instruct Excel that the With---End With statement has now ended.

7. The Second With-End With Statement

You have already learned about the operation of the With-End With statement in the previous steps. The code provided does have two such statements, so now the second With-End With statement will be discussed. As you have judged by now, this statement is performing the relevant action to create the macros. The action that it is executing is of changing the color of the font to blue. You can also see that this statement is a lot shorter than the first one. Based on the general structure it displays, each line will now be explained.

- **The First Line (With Selection.Font.):** It starts by opening the statement with the With command, which provides Excel with instructions to follow the subsequent statements for the defined object appearing there. The object being discussed in the statement is "Selection.Font." As per previous discussions, Selection is the current choice for the written macro code. This choice of object being mentioned in the statement is the active cell. Furthermore, the Font refers to the font of the text in the active cell. Thus, "Selection.Font" is indicating the active cell's text font. With the "With Selection.Font" command, Excel is following the necessary instructions on the active cell text font.

- **The Second Line (.Color = -4165632):** This particular line of code is also instructing Excel about the color of choice. In this case the color chosen is an absolute color, as the relevant value for the color has been provided in the macro. The code represents the blue color, which will be chosen for the text font in the active cell.

- **The Third Line (TintAndShade = 0):** This statement is also similar to the one in the previous With-End With command. With it, Excel will keep a neutral color for the chosen shade, which is neither light nor dark. With the "TintAndShade" command, the lightening or darkening can be changed. But, the value given is zero, which makes the shade a neutral color, which means it does not lightens nor darkens for the active cell text font.

- **The Fourth Line (End With):** Just like before, this statement ends the With statement. Thus, any code that follows this statement is irrelevant to the With-End With command.

8. EndSub

This statement marks the end of the sub procedure chosen for this particular macro code. As soon as Excel compiles this statement, it is instructed that the macro has now terminated. Beyond this statement, no line of code exists to be executed.

Useful Tips For Understanding Macros

If you really feel like learning macros in Excel at a faster pace, then these tips will definitely help you to improve your efficiency and speed. For understanding these tips better, you can use the code example mentioned in the previous section of this chapter as a reference.

- **Tip 1: Modify various VBA macro code portions to keep learning new aspects:**

  As an example for this tip, you can modify the statement "ActiveCell.FormulaR1C1 = "This is an easy Excel tutorial" and change it to "ActiveCell.FormulaR1C1 = "MS Excel is easy!" You will see that the statement being filled in the active cell, as per the code will now change to the new text.

Similarly, you can also experiment with the colors selected for the font and interior of the active cell. For example, change the value of the color from 255 to 155 and the other color value from -4165632 to 185. You can see the changes in the colors yourself.

- **Tip 2: Try removing some of the statements from the code to see how it influences the complete macro:**

As an example, what changes might occur if you remove the statement: "Selection.Columns.AutoFit"? Surely, your text in the column's active cell will not be completely fitted within the cell. You can have a look at such changes by running the Excel macros again after modifying it. Just use the short cut key combination: "Ctrl + Shift + B" and have a look at the result yourself. You will find that the changes made using the above two tips will alter the result you had from the previous macro code. Thus, modifying like this will help you understand how the code works more efficiently.

- **Tip 3: Keep repeating and practicing the steps that you learn:**

Mastering macros is the easiest when you practice it regularly. Repeating your exercises, and practicing new codes will give you the upper hand in understand how it functions. Make sure you follow the example provided in the previous section. Do look for more such examples through various sources and study how each of the command function to modify the worksheet. A good way of practicing is by keeping a real time view of the editor screen beside your code window so that you can see the changes made through your macro code there only. You may need a dual-monitor setup for maximum efficiency in this case.

- **Tip 4: Keep studying for it and read various sources:**

Find genuine sources that teach you about Excel macros besides this book. Note that this book is covering a basic understanding of how macros work. For practicing exercises and examples, you can register yourself on authentic web portals that are dedicated to Excel macros. You can even join forums supporting this coding language to ask your queries whenever you have while practicing.

CHAPTER 10

Optimization Of VBA Code
For Quicker Approach To Macros

This chapter will cover the improvement and optimization introduction and techniques for you to practice. These practical techniques are great to strengthen your basics as a VBA programmer. Moreover, you can easily be counted among expert programmers if you are capable of optimizing your macro code.

With optimized VBA codes, you are saving a lot of your time, which is why you will now learn various ways of optimizing your code. Note that, you will have to understand each of the following methods religiously and implement them in your programming to create automation, dashboards, and Excel reports.

1. Logic Analyzation

Planning to optimize your code before even understanding the logic behind it is a bad move. So, you need to first understand why you are performing such an action on your macro. Without the relevant logic behind it, there may never be a significant value added to a written VBA program. Streamlining a code requires a logic behind it, which in return will offer you a high-performing macro.

2. Switch off the updating screen

You should avoid repainting or flickering of your screen, which can be bothersome while working on a code. You can do this with the following code:

Application.ScreenUpdating = False 'This will switch off the updating at the starting of your code.

Application.ScreenUpdating = False 'This will switch on the updating after the code has ended.

3. Switch of the calculations carried out automatically

When there is a change in the number or content of the currently active cell, the formulae assigned to such a cell will also change. This results in high volatility in the calculations in the cell, as the complete data starts recalculating automatically. It can result in a lower performance, as you may not need the data to be calculated at that moment. For that, you can turn of the calculations being carried out using the following code:

Appllication.Calculation = xlCalculationManual ' This will switch of the calculations at the starting of the code.

Application.Calculation = xlCalculationAutomatic ' This will switch the calculation back on after the code ends.

After that, when you need to implement the logic of the program to calculate the data using the formulae (as the macros is dependent on the formulae), you will need to implement the code below:

ActiceSheet.Calculate ' This will calculate the filled formulae in the currently active worksheet.

Application.Calculate ' This will calculate the data using the formulae for all the workbooks currently active in Excel.

4. Disabling the Events

You can use the following code to stop the events from reducing the performance of the macros.

Application.EnableEvents

You can instruct the processor of the VBA language to fire the events. As there is a rare chance of firing of events during the modification of a code, you may not need it active at the moment. So, it is better to turn them off and increase the performance of the macro code.

5. Hiding the page breaks

When you are using the latest MS Excel version to execute the VBA macros, it may take longer to execute than normal. This will cause them to take more time than the previous versions of Excel. In fact, the macros that need several seconds to accomplish a task in the previous versions of Excel will need several minutes to fulfill in the latest versions. This can occur when some of the conditions become active. To make it run more efficiently, you can disable the page breaks that occur while writing the code. This can be done using:

ActiveSheet.DisplayPageBreaks = False

6. Utilizing the "With" command while processing objects

When a user is trying to retrieve the methods and properties of an object within multiple lines of code, he or she will have to avoid using the name of the object. Plus, he or she will also have to avoid utilizing the complete path of the object over and over. This can cause the VBA processor to reduce in performance as it has to use complete compilation for the object every time it runs through it. This is similar to what macros have been designed to do. Think of a user who has to perform the same task repeatedly. Your VBA program may also not like this action. Thus, we use "With" statement to make things faster. Here is an example of a slow and fast macro covering the With statement.

Example of a Slow Macro:

Sheets(1).Range("A1:E1").Font.Italic = True

Sheets(1).Range("A1:E1").Font.Interior.Color = vbRed

Sheets(1).Range("A1:E1").MergeCells = True

Example of a Fast Macro:

With Sheets(1).Range("A1:E1").Font.Italic = True

.Font.Interior.Color = vbRed

.MergeCells = True

End With

The importance of understanding the two macro codes is that, while both perform the same task, the faster macro is using the "With" statement. This statement engages in minimum object qualification for the code. This increases the performance of the code as there is less data to be compiled in it. With this statement, you do not have to write the complete concept comprising of Range, etc.

7. Instead of dual double quotes, you should use vbNullString

This command is a little faster compared to the use of double quotes. This is because vbNullString acts as a constant that has zero bytes of memory. On the other hand, double quotes is a string that has a memory of 4 – 6 bytes, that can cause a little more processing while dealing with a macros. For example:

Instead of using *strVariable = ""* , you can use *strVariable = vbNullString.*

8. Free the object variable memory they are using

When an object is created in a macro code, the program creates two memories for it. These are a pointer and an object. The pointer is also called as a reference for the object. You may hear it from experts that VB does not require pointers, but it is not the case. The truth is that VB uses pointers but does not allow a user to change them. At the backend, the program keeps using pointers as well.

To remove the object in Visual Basic, you can change its value as null. However, this arises a question: If the program is continuously utilizing object pointers, how can its value be changed to null? The answer to it cannot be removed. Upon setting the pointer value to null, a process known as garbage collector comes into play. This program chooses to destroy the object or leave it be. You can authorize this garbage collector in multiple ways. However, VB utilizes a way known as Pointer count method. In this process, once Visual Basic is done analyzing the last line of code where the object is set to null, it moves the pointer that is existing. At that particular time, there are no assigned pointers to that object. At that moment, the garbage collector removes the object and destroys all its active resources. If, however, there is a pointer referencing to the same object, it will not be removed.

9. Reduce the number of lines with the help of colon (:)

It is prudent to avoid using multiple statements individually, when you can still join them together to create a single line. You can understand this by the following examples:

Example of Slow Macro:

With Selection.WrapText = True

.ShrinkToFit = False

End With

Example of Fast Macro:

With Selection.WrapText = True:.ShrinkToFit = False

End With

As you can witness from the examples given above, several statements can be joined together when you use the colon symbol. After implementing it in the code, you can witness a reduction in the readability as well as the speed for the written code.

For the faster code, the logic behind it that is compiled is:

Upon saving the macro, it is compiled digitally. Compared to the one that is readable by a human and found in the VB editor, the keywords used take up a token of 3 byte. You cannot use keywords as variables. Plus, keywords process at a much faster rate as these are understood by the computer much better. The literal strings, variables, and comments on the contrary are not directives or keywords. These are saved in the code as they are. A VBA compiling tool will tokenize the words, but will not do the same to the lines. Plus, these lines are not shortened and stays as they are. These also end with a carriage return (meaning resetting the position of the line of code).

Upon execution of a VBA macro, the processor compiles each line one at a time. Each token of the line being compiled is then saved with the help of digital compilers. Then the processes of interpretation and execution follow. After that, the process moves on to the next line after it. With the use of a colon to join several lines into one, there is a reduction in the processes occurring to fetch the data by the VBA program, thus improving speed and performance.

The modification will end up improving the code. Moreover, there is a limit of using just 255 characters in one line. You may not have an efficient debugging process with the help of F8 key. Thus, it is not advisable to write long single lines, just to make the code more readable, which will only sacrifice the speed and performance.

10. Declaring multiple constants as Constant and several variables as Variable

It may seem a pretty obvious tip to utilize in your code, but many users do not follow this. For instance:

Dim Pi As Double

Pi = 3.14159

Instead of this, you can use,

Const Pi As Double

Pi = 3.14159

As the value of Pi does not change, its evaluation will be processed during the compiling process, which is unlike the processing of other variables. Other variables require processing multiple times.

11. Do not Copy Paste codes Unnecessarily

Copying and pasting codes can be bad for a code's performance. You can optimize your code without the need of copy pasting various steps with the following tips:

Avoid this:

Sheet1.Range("A1:A200").CopySheet2.Range("B1").PasteSpecial

Application.CutCopyMode = False   'Clear Cliboard

Instead, use this:

'Bypassing the clipboard

Sheet1.Range("A1:A200").CopyDestination: =
Sheet2.Range("B1")

Avoid This:

Sheet1.Range("A1:A200").CopySheet2.Range("B1").PasteS
pecialxlPasteValues

Application.CutCopyMode = False   'Clear Cliboard

Instead, Use this:

'Bypassing the clipboard, if there is a need for only values

Sheet2.Range("B1:B200").Value =
Sheet1.Range("A1:A200").Value

Avoid This:

Sheet1.Range("A1:A200").CopySheet2.Range("B1").PasteS
pecialxlPasteFormulas

Application.CutCopyMode = False   'Clear Cliboard

Instead, use this:

'Bypassing the clipboard, if there is a need of formulas

Sheet2.Range("B1:B200").Formula =
Sheet1.Range("A1:A200").Formula

'You can apply a similar code with Array formulas and FormulaR1C1.

12. Utilizing the functions in the worksheets instead of creating your own logic

While it may seem logical to develop and use something that the user understands better, it may not be the case for Excel as well. It is always prudent to use the native codes provided in the worksheet so that the code can be processed at a much faster rate. Using *Application.WorkSheetFunction* is instructing the VBA processor to utilize the codes present natively in the function sheet instead of the interpreted ones. Your Visual Basic Application will have an easier time understanding the code that is already present in the sheets for it to use.

Here is an example for it:

mProduct

Application.WorksheetFunction.Product(Range("C7:C14"))

Rather than using your own logic to define the code, like:

mProduct = 1

For i = 7 to 14

*mProduct = mProduct * Cells(4,i)*

Next

13. Replace statements like "Indexed For" with "For Each"

When a code is involving a looping sequence, you should avoid using the statement "Indexed For". Here is an example of the modification of the above code to explain this:

For Each myCel in Range("C7:C14")

mProduct = mProduct * myCell.Value

Next

This is related to the qualification of objects and works in a similar way as a "With" statement.

14. Avoid using "Macro Recorder" similar to a code

Using this code will help in improving performance of your macro. Here is an example to explain it better:

Avoid this:

Range("A1").Select

Selection.Interior.Color = vbRed

Instead, use this:

[A1].Interior.Color = vbRed

Peppering your code with statements like "Selection" and "Select" is going to cause reduction in performance for your macro. You need to understand the reason behind going to cell and modifying its properties, when you can simply use the latter command to change it there only.

15. Do not use variants and objects in the statement of declaration

After focusing on a prudent logic, make sure you are avoiding the use of variants and objects in the declaration statements. For instance:

Avoid using:

Dim mCell As Object or

Dim i As Variant

By specifying the type or value of a variable, you are helping the macro save extra memory. This can have a greater benefit when dealing with objects that are larger in size. It can be confusing to remember the exact entity that you had declared as a variant. This can result in misusing the variable when the value is being assigned to it. In fact, Excel might typecast it without showing any syntax errors.

Furthermore, the descriptor for the variant is 16 bytes in length, the integer is 2 bytes in length, long is 4 bytes in length, and double is 8 bytes in length. Misusing these can have a drastic impact on the code's performance. Instead, you can use:

Dim I As Long

Instead of

Dim I As Variant

Similarly:

Avoid using:

Dim mCell As Object 'or

Dim mSheet As Object

Instead, use:

Dim mCell As Range 'or

Dim mSheet As Worksheet

16. Direct Declaration of OLE Objects

Declaring and defining Object Linking and Embedding (OLE) objects in the statement of declaration is known as "Early Binding." On the other hand, declaring and defining objects is known as "Late Binding." Note that it is always prudent to choose Early Binding over Late one. For example:

Avoid using:

Dim oXL As Object

Set oXL = CreateObject("Excel.Application")

Instead, use:

Dim oXL As Excel.Application

CHAPTER 11

Tips And Shortcuts For Excel Macros And VBA Codes

Macros Keyboard Shortcut Assignment

In this chapter, let us take into view 2 varying ways for developing keyboard shortcuts to execute macros. In addition, you will also learn about the pros and cons of both the methods for shortcut keys.

With the assignment of keyboard shortcuts, you are reducing the time it take to type the code and process it during its execution in Excel. This is generally applicable when there is a need to perform various actions in repetition. In this chapter, you will see how the two methods will use the shortcut keys to utilize the speed and efficiency of the program. These two ways will now be discussed one by one.

The First Method: The Window For Macro Options:

With the help of the macro options window, you can create shortcut keys for running various macros from time to time. You can find the instruction to set these up below:

1. You can start this by finding the Develop tab option and then pressing the button highlighted as macros. You can check the instructions provided in one of the previous chapters to

enable your Developer tab option if it is not visible in the Ribbon. You can also use the short key combination: Alt + F8 for enabling the Developer tab.

2. Upon choosing the macro to which you are looking to assign the shortcut key, press the Options button.

3. In the pop-up window for Macros Options, you can create the shortcut you want to add for it by pressing a number, symbol, or a letter. You need to beware of not overriding the shortcuts that existing beforehand. Some shortcuts are already existing, like Ctrl + V for pasting. To avoid overriding any existing shortcut keys, you can join your selected number, symbol, or letter with a shift key as well. This will make the combination a little complex, but it will not be overridden. So, the code can become Ctrl + Shift + V.

To delete an existing shortcut key, you need to first access the Macro options window just like in the previous steps. After that, you just have the delete the symbol, letter, or number assigned in the box there.

The Second Method: Application.OnKey The VBA Method:

With the help of VBA code, you can create shortcuts for your macros. The statement that you can use for this is the "Application.OnKey." This statement can help in removing and creating shortcuts. Plus, it will feature a number of options, which are more flexible than the macro option method. You need to first start it by using the Visual Basic editor. For this, just press the VB button of the Developer option tab. You can also use the shortcut key combination: Alt + F11.

Using OnKey to create shortcuts

In this technique using VB editor, a code will be written to assign the keyboard shortcuts to their respective macros.

First, you will need to develop a macro and name it properly, such as CreateShortcut. After that, you will then begin a new line with the command statement "Application.OnKey." This statement will follow a space. Note that there are two parameters in the Application.OnKey technique. The first one is for the procedure, and the second one is for the key.

Here, the key is the shortcut key combination on the keyboard. On the other hand, the procedure is macro name that is called upon typing the key combination. You need to enclose both parameters within quotes.

Check out this example to learn it better:

Sub CreateShortcut() 'Name of the macro

Application.OnKey *"+^{V}",* *"CellColorBlue"* 'This happens when you press the combination later while running the macro

End Sub

In the above example, you can see that the combination shortcut has been described as "+^{C}". This is the key parameter being used in the macro code. Note that + sign is code that is used for Ctrl, and ^sign is used for Shift. Plus, V is the key that has been added in braces. You can find the complete list of codes for all the key combinations through online sources. Using this code, you are naming the procedure and assigning it to the relevant key combination. The above code example is using the key combination to execute a macro known as "CellColorBlue."

Deleting key combination shortcuts with the help of OnKey

For this check out the code first:

Sub DeleteShortcut()

Application.OnKey "+^{V}"

End Sub

You can figure out that the code used for deleting the shortcut key is easy. It looks quite similar, with little modification to the one for creating the key combination. Instead of adding "CreateShortcut", this code adds "DeleteShortcut". Plus, you can notice that the name of the procedure has also been removed. Removing it is instructing Excel that there is no need to assign any combination strokes on the keyboard to perform an action. Plus, it is a command that is resetting the combinations on the keyboard to their default setting in Excel. For example, if you use the Ctrl + V combination, it will process the computer to perform a pasting action when the keys are pressed.

The techniques for deleting and creating macros have several code lines when utilizing the OnKey technique. It will let you assign shortcuts for various macros and that too all at once.

Using automatic OnKey setup with events:

Such processes of assigning shortcut key combinations can also be automated using the events Workbook_BeforeClose and Workbook_Open. You can do that with the help of the following instructions:

1. Find the Project Window in the Visual BasIC Editor window, and double click to open an existing workbook.

2. Choose the Workbook from the menu dropping down.

3. It will include the event Workbook_Open. After that, add the code line for a created macro. For this, let's assume that the code for calling the macro is "CallModule1.CreateShortcut". Note that the code will not have the quotes. In addition, you can even delete the macro by adding another event for closing the workbook at any instance. For that, you need to choose BeforeClose from the drop-down option present on the right-hand side of the window. After that you can call the macro.

If the storage of the macros is in a personal workbook, you can stick to the same procedure as discussed in the previous steps. You can look for online sources to study the creation of a personal workbook for macro. You can also learn about the advantages they have.

The Pros And Cons Of The Two Methods

For the two methods, you can utilize keyboard shortcuts for each file that you open in Excel. This is true for the time the file that has the macro stays open. Here is a list of the pros and cons for both the methods now:

Pros of Macro Options Window:

Setting up the keyboard shortcuts using macro options is quite easy. For the ones who feel that writing a program to create a macro shortcut is tough, this method is a boon.

Cons of Macro Options:

1. Several limitations exist when it comes to the usage of keys or key combinations. Some keys that cannot be used for shortcuts are Page Up, End, Home, etc.

2. Another issue that can arise in Macro options method is that a key may already be assigned to another shortcut. So, if you are a developer, your assigned key combinations may not

control the execution of certain tasks that the user processes. Assigning key and overriding them may create confusions for the user and the developer. Plus, the order of operation for the macro names is alphabetically. This is because the macro names present in the open workbooks are present on the computer of the user.

3. No index exists for the shortcut keys using this method. You cannot look at them in a specific directory or archive. Thus, if you have already created several of them and you cannot keep track of them, then it can be difficult for you to use them. You do have macros that can help you keep track of the created shortcuts, but that will only consume more time for you to prepare one.

Pros Of Application.OnKey Technique:

1. It is easier to find a keyboard shortcut with the help of a VBA code with the keyword OnKey. You can implement the use of the Ctrl + F combination that will open the find window for searching in the Visual Basic Editor.

2. If several macros or workbooks are using the same shortcuts, you may order or prioritize the executing macros. The shortcuts that are developed with the help of the OnKey technique are prioritized compared to the ones that are created using Macro Options. Thus, executing the technique using OnKey will ensure that the shortcut key created using it is run before other options.

3. You can use the delete or remove action with much ease for keyboard shortcuts in this method. You may have to create macro keys for disabling and enabling them from the Ribbon using the keyboard. Another way of doing so is by using one shortcut on the keyboard to toggle multiple shortcuts on the keyboard.

4. You can also use certain special buttons that may not be usable in the Macro options method. These buttons include Page Down, End, Alt, Home, etc. In addition, the combined keys Alt + Ctrl will offer various options for shortcut keys.

5. Depending on the various workbook conditions, the shortcuts can modify the procedures dynamically.

Cons of Application.OnKey Technique

1. With a modification in the macro name, the code will also need to be revised.

2. You will have to be present to process the action for the assignment of shortcuts and execute them.

Thus, you have been briefed about the two methods for assigning shortcuts for macros. Which method do you think is more suitable for you? Surely, any expert developer who uses macros is going to choose the OnKey technique as it is more efficient in multiple ways. Plus, it offers the ability to find the shortcuts in a much easier way. It also has more options for the key combinations, and has a decent control over disabling and enabling the shortcut keys (even for multiple shortcuts at once using toggle macro).

But, note that even this method is flawed in some ways. So, there is no perfect method, and you will have to decide for yourself to choose the one that makes you most comfortable. Nevertheless, try to master the OnKey method as it will give you better benefits than Macro options method.

Some Important Excel Macros Shortcuts That You Can Learn

Now, we will go through some shortcuts and tips that you can utilize in your Excel workbooks for saving time. Using these for macros and other applications related to MS Office will give you a head start while working. Note that this section will discuss some of those shortcuts and tips to help you out, but that does not mean that these are the only ones. You can find more through online research for VBA and Macros shortcuts.

That said, let us start:

1. **Alt + F11 (Opens the VBE window):** The editor window for Visual Basic or VBE can be opened using this shortcut key. As you already know, VBE is used for creating forms for users and writing macros. You can also click the Visual Basic button present in the Developer Tab option in Excel. Choosing the shortcut key is faster and more efficient. Similarly, you can use a similar combination key for Mac PCs. But, the only change is that the key combination has an Opt instead of Alt. So, the key shortcut is Fn + Opt + F11 or Opt + F11. For enabling the Developer tab option in your Ribbon, you can look for the instructions discussed in one of the previous sections of this book.

2. **Ctrl + Space (completes words automatically):** This key action is one of the most widely used among developers of VBA. While using the codes, the Ctrl + Space key combination will open a dropdown menu that incorporates constants, variables, properties, methods, and objects.

   In addition, you can implement the Ctrl_Space shortcut using your Visual Basic editor as well. For that you can do the following:

   • Start by typing a code statement, like ActiveCell.

   • Once you type the first few keys, press the Ctrl + Space keys.

   • You will see a dropdown for a group of all the words in VBA that start with the word Act.

- You can use the down and up arrow keys to choose the word you want to use.

- After that you can press Enter or Tab to select the word and complete it automatically.

You get two important pros with this shortcut key. Besides being great supporters in saving your time while you are using the debug action for your codes, these will:

- Save time for you without the need of typing long variables or words.

- Curb any chances of unnecessary typos while typing the code.

3. **The Function Keys On Laptops:** If you have been using a keyboard of a laptop to write the code, then you may have felt the need of pressing the Fn key for pressing the Function keys, like F11. Note that there are multiple uses of a function key on your laptop, for which the Fn key needs to be pressed in combination with the keys from F1 – F12. Several laptops come with a feature where the Fn can be locked. This causes the Function keys to act as the primary keys, so they do not need to be pressed with the Fn key to activate.

4. **Worksheet Intellisense Menu:** The Intellisense menu is a drop down menu comprising of words that are predefined for your help. Upon typing the period symbol (.), you can see this menu activating in the editor of Visual Basic. However, it does not always work. A case where it does not work is while working with property of worksheets. If you press Worksheets("Sheet1"), it will not show up the Intellisense menu. This can frustrate some users, as they may think that it is some kind of a glitch.

However, this happens because the worksheets property consists of various references to multiple sheets. Based on the references, methods and properties varying for each of the cases. Note that the Intellisense is not so intelligent that it can identify the period symbol there. This frustration has to be coped with until some update comes in the application to deal with it. Nevertheless, you can use the following two ways to avoid this issue and find the Intellisense dropdown menu for worksheets as well.

- You can use the worksheets codename that you are referencing. This technique is quite easy as it can help in bringing the menu out. This works because the code does not break if the user wishes to change the name of the sheet.

- The second way is by first setting the worksheet you want to work on as a variable in the Worksheets object. After that, whenever you will type the name of the variable assigned to your worksheet, with a period after that, it will show up the Intellisense menu.

5. **Free Use of Comments:** As explained earlier, comments can be helpful in understanding the created or modified codes in a macro. It also helps in understanding the purpose of a code in the macro. It was explained earlier that a comment can be started with the apostrophe mark ('). As soon as you move the cursor away from the comment line, the text in the line will change to green color. That way, you will know that it is a comment and it will be easier for you to differentiate it with the rest of the code. Note that VBA will avoid reading all comments that are starting with the apostrophe mark. There is no limit to the usage of comments in the editor window.

But, note that comments are still not that widely used by expert VBA developers. They believe that the code itself is able to give full explanation of what the code is doing. So, they believe that adding a comment is useless. However, this may not be applicable to all types of users. Beginners can get help with visible comments to understand the code. Some other reasons for the significance of comments are:

- Upon arriving back to an existing piece of macro code later, it is possible that you may not remember the purpose of a created macro. With comments, you can at least provide various sections of the code with headings that will define their purpose. It makes it quite easy, at least for cases where the macro code is lengthy. In addition, it will help in utilizing the complete code at any time at a much faster rate.

- Sometimes, users or developers share their VB project codes with other developers or users for various objectives. For the person who has not written the code, it can be a great advantage to understand what the code is doing with the help of mentioned comments.

6. **Using F8 For Stepping Via Each Code Line:** For stepping through every code line, we use the keyboard key F8. This shortcut key is applicable in Mac computers with the combination: Cmd + Shift + I. With this shortcut key, you can debug and test each code line in your created macros. Additionally, you can access Excel along with the editor screen to check the performance of each line executing on the screen. This is more feasible when you use a dual-monitor system.

This can be of great advantage in situations where you want to keep testing each line for errors side by side. For using the Through or Step Into shortcut, you can follow the below steps:

- Click within the macro you want to execute. You can click on the code line that you want to step into. The line will start at the top.

95

- Press the F8 key.

- It will highlight the macro name in yellow color.

- Press F8 again after it to compile the code line. This will then highlight the line after it.

- Keep pressing the F8 key to compile each line.

Note that the lines that are highlighted on every step are not executed until the F8 key is pressed again.

7. **Assigning Macros To Various Shapes:** It may seem an outdated layout for using sheet controls for various buttons that run macros. Fortunately, the use of shapes is also applicable in Excel to execute macros. You can format or color these shapes to make them look like buttons in your sheet. Here is the method to assign various shapes to your macros:

- Add a shape on your sheet. Format it the way you prefer it. You can change the shape to circular or rectangular as per your preference.

- After that, press right click on the shape you selected and click on the "Assign Macro" option.

- Select the relevant macro that you want from the list provided and press OK. Normally, this macro is the same one that is stored with the same shape as you have decided for yours to be.

- Click the shape by selecting a cell from your worksheet.

- When you move your mouse cursor over the shape, you will see that your mouse cursor changes to a hand. This indicates that you can perform an action with the shape. In this case it will execute the macro assigned to it.

Note that it is prudent that you have a message box option present there with a Yes or No button to ask you if you want to run the macro. This is helpful in preventing the execution of an unnecessary macro.

8. **Utilize the For Next Loop For Running Repetitive Tasks Automatically:** Excel macros have been designed for a significant purpose, which is to perform tasks that need to be repeated again and again. Such tasks include copying workbook data from one to multiple workbooks, setting up filters for every pivot table, developing lists in sheets, formatting several sheets, etc. Note that loops are of high significance in VB applications. Their purpose is to automatically run certain tasks assigned to them. It helps in looping a certain set of instruction until the tasks fulfills the purpose completely.

As mentioned earlier, several types of loops exist that have been used in various programming languages. The For Next loop is the most common of them all. You can learn about loops in detail from various online sources.

9. **Utilizing Option Explicit:** Many developers avoid using it, but it is still a recommended tip that you can use for its advantages. You can use Option Explicit for declaring variables. It is a way of preventing typos for various variable names in the VBE. Declaring variables and avoiding unnecessary tokenizing has already been discussed in previous chapters.

With Option Explicit, you are instructing VBA to develop a variable and save it within the memory to make it accessible at later stages while running a code. As variables are saved beforehand, you can use the variable without making any typos and save some time while writing the code and repeating the variable name. Any undeclared variable will be prompted by the VBE with a compiler error that says "Variable Not Defined." It will also show the undeclared variable so that you can fix the typo without the need of searching for it. If your Option Explicit function is turned off, you may still end up with errors upon typing a misspelled variable. But, it can be difficult to locate the error in a lengthy macro without Option Explicit function turned on. So, try using it while you write your code. To turn it on, just type "Option Explicit" on the top of the module. VBE may automate it for you if you go to Tools -> Options -> and ticking the "Require Variable Declaration" box. You can see the words Option Explicit written on top of your module for writing the code to know that it is turned on.

10. **Utilizing the Excel Tables or ListObjects:** Several advantages exist that support the effective role of Excel Tables in workbooks. You can reduce the amount of time spent with these by automatically filling columns, sourcing data for pivot tables, and formatting them. With Excel tables, the VBA code is much easier to write specifically for dynamic data. We refer to it as dynamic, as it keeps updating itself depending upon the addition of new data set or list in the row or columns of the worksheets. You can have plenty of instances where the use of Excel tables is needed. For that ListObjects is used in the code to create the necessary operation for modifying the table as you progress with the data input. Note that Excel tables let you update the list even when a data is removed from the list in the table.

11. **Using Macro Recorder:** This feature is unique to Excel and VBA applications. Upon running it, it will start creating VBA code in MS Excel. For instance, upon turning it on, you can perform your usual tasks in Excel, like writing formulae or copy/pasting text. Meanwhile, Macro recorder will start creating the relevant code for your actions and save it to the module for code in the project window.

This outstanding tool is great for beginners as it helps in understanding how the code is being created for your macro actions. It gives you snippets of the code and understanding from time to time. Note that the object model of Excel is so vast that it is almost impossible to learn all the methods, object references, and properties present in it. Thus, using a Macro recorder can help in accessing some of the code for your objects, shapes, lists, slicers, pivot tables, etc., that you frequently use in your workbooks.

However, there are some restrictions with Macro recorders. It will not add any code snippets for message boxes, If commands, errors/typos, loops, etc. For those, the user will have to create the code on his or her own by learning these advanced methods. These methods will enable you to understand the complete VB coding language for creating macros efficiently.

12. **Immediate Window:** This window lets Visual Basic editor to execute each code line separately. You have the ability to execute a technique related to an object or return the code output on the Immediate Window. For instance, you have a task to locate the number of worksheets in a particular workbook. For that, you can ask the window a question in VBA code, like:

?Worksheets.Count

Upon pressing enter, your query gets addressed with its answer in the following line. You can also use Immediate Window for debugging code lines with the help of Debug.Print technique. Furthermore, you can access this window with the shortcut key: Ctrl + G.

13. **Macros Keyboard Shortcuts Assignment:** You are already familiar with this technique, as it had been discussed in one of the previous chapters. Nevertheless, it does not hurt to revisit it once again as it is an important function to help you assign

shortcuts for your created macros. You can use the Macro Options window to access the area for assigning the key for it.

- Press the button for Macros located in the Developer option or you can also access it from the View option present in the ribbon.

- Select the file that consists of the macro from the dropdown menu present in the Macros Options box.

- Select the macros from the list and press the button saying "Options."

- Type the letter for which you want to assign your developed macros. As mentioned earlier, you can create a complex combination to avoid any overriding of the shortcut keys for some other operation. It is always advisable to select a key with the Shift key to make it a unique combination.

- Press the OK button once you have assigned the keys.

- After that, you can access your macros by pressing the shortcut key linked to it and use it.

14. **Checking Whether A Selected Range Is Present Or Not:** Several times, you may face a situation where a range of cells have to be identified whether they are selected or not. This is needed to be done prior to running a macro. In some situations, they may have a shape, like a slicer, a chart, etc., selected for them, then it can cause an error in the macro code.

For example, a code is there to delete rows that are blank in a chosen range of cells. For running a macro normally, you will have to first choose a range for the code to work. The following code will help in verifying whether the range is chosen or not:

'For checking if a range is chosen

If TypeName(Selection) <> "Range" Then MsgBox "Please choose a range beforehand.", vbOKOnly, "Select Range"

Exit Sub

End If

In this code, a name of the object or data type will be returned by the function TypeName for the provided objects or variables. In the above case, it will check for the Selection and return the object types selected there. If a range is not selected, then the If statement will serve its purpose. Usually, this code needs to be added above the macro. If there is no range selected, then a pop-up box appears on the screen that will suggest the user to first select a range. As usual, the Exit Sub statement will end the macro.

15. **Ctrl + Y (Deletes a Code Line):** This useful tool in VBE is there to remove any lines that your editor cursor is actively highlighting. This can be a little confusing for some, as Ctrl + Y is a shortcut key that has been universally used for redoing an operation in an application, even in Excel. If you check the menu for Edit in your Excel, you will see that the Redo command does not have any shortcut key assigned to it. Alternatively, for Redo, you can use Alt + R or Alt + E for redoing. However, in the VBE editor, you can use Ctrl + Y to delete a line.

16. **Using Ctrl + i To Access Quick Info:** This significant keyboard shortcut is there to help with various tips and short notes on what the various methods, functions, and properties are used for. To use it, you can press the Ctrl + i buttons, which you can do like this:

- Highlight the cursor on the relevant text or word that you want to look information for.

- After that, press the Ctrl + i keys.

- You will then see a screen next to the text.

- You can press the Esc button to close the window or you can simply move your cursor from that text.

If there is a variable chosen within the code line that you wish to see information for (specifically for its parameters, instead of the variable's value or the type of data it has), then you can press the key combination Ctrl + Shift + i to look at the information for the parameter.

17. **Ctrl + j For Using Intellisense dropdown menu:** Intellisense menu was discussed previously so you know what it is used for. You can use it for displaying methods, objects, properties, etc. after you type the period symbol (.). However, sometimes you want to revisit a particular line to view the Intellisense menu for that particular object. For that you can press the Ctrl + J keys to view the menu. Alternatively, you can simply type that line again to reopen the Intellisense menu for that particular line.

Furthermore, you can press the combination keys Ctrl + J to choose the various variables from the dropdown list. Sometimes, a user may select a wrong variable, for which he or she needs to alter the name. Pressing the Ctrl + J keys will offer a list of variable names for that when the cursor is highlighted over that particular mistyped variable. In addition, prefixing a variable name will close the other variable from the list.

18. **Worksheet Functions:** Several functions in the worksheet can also be utilized in your workbook in Excel. You can use these functions in various formulae in Excel, like min, max, countif,

vlookup, match, etc. For this, you need to type WorksheetFunction., in the editor for macro, and you can then view all the functions that are provided to you in Visual Basic applications.

You can think of worksheet functions as a live example that shows how the efficiency of Excel combines with the usability of VBA code. Note that upon using it, you will be provided with the list of arguments, but not their names. So, you will have to type the formula for it in Excel to determine the type of argument, unless you have already memorized them.

While it may vary from user to user, yet Match is the most prominently used function of worksheet in VBA. It can be used for finding a value and returning a column or row number that this matched value indicates. For some, it can be an easier alternative to Range.Find technique.

Understanding Absolute and Relative Macro Recording

Now that you have attuned yourself to the basics of Macros and got a little glimpse of Macro recording, it is now time to delve a little deeper. We are now going to understand how you can begin recording macros.

Before you get started, let us understand an essential point: Excel provides you with two modes for the purpose of recording. These two modes are absolute reference and relative reference.

Let us try to find out how we can work these two modes.

Mode One: Recording with Absolute References

By default, you will be using absolute reference when you start working with recording macros. When we use the term 'absolute reference', then we are using it in the context of cell references that are discovered in formulas. What this means is that when a cell reference in a particular formula has an absolute reference, then it does not modify itself automatically when you paste the cell into a new area of the Excel sheet.

Perhaps the best way to understand this is by actually putting the entire concept into practice. So let us get right to it.

Let us first create a chart in excel.

	A	B	C	D	E	F	G	H
1		**Region**	**Target**	**Branch**				
2		USA	New York	01234				
3		USA	New York	12341				
4		USA	New York	23544				
5		USA	New York	73568				
6		Asia	Shanghai	94678				
7		Asia	Shanghai	25208				
8		Asia	Shanghai	24621				
9								

Now let us get down to recording the macro.

1. The first thing that you should make sure is that you have the A1 cell selected.

2. Head over to the Developer tab and then select Record Macro.

3. You will now be prompted to give a name for the macro. For the purpose of this example, we are going to go right ahead and name the macro as "AddTotal". Not very imaginative, but if you like, we could also go with "TotalRecall". It's your choice.

4. Next, select This Workbook for the location of the save.

5. Then click on OK to begin recording. From this point onwards, Excel is going to record everything you do. So let us get started on the below steps.

6. Select cell A9 and enter 'Total' into the field.

7. Once you have entered Total into A9, select the cell D9 and then type this formula: =COUNTA(D2:D8). This gives you a total of the branch numbers in the box that you have selected (which would be D9). The reason why we use COUNTA is because the branch numbers are actually stored as text.

8. Now head back to the Developer tab and select the Stop Recording option to stop the recording process.

Now the final sheet should look something like the below:

	A	B	C	D	E	F	G	H
1		**Region**	**Target**	**Branch**				
2		USA	New York	01234				
3		USA	New York	12341				
4		USA	New York	23544				
5		USA	New York	73568				
6		Asia	Shanghai	94678				
7		Asia	Shanghai	25208				
8		Asia	Shanghai	24621				
9	Total			7				

Now here is where the incredible happens. If you would like to view your macro, then all you have to do is delete the total row (which would be Row 9). Then you simply have to follow the below steps:

1. Go to the Developer tab and then select Macros

2. You should now look for the "AddTotal" macro (or the "TotalRecall" macro, depending on how you named it).

3. When you find it, click on the run button.

If everything goes well with Excel, you should now be able to see your actions played back. You will notice that your table will now have a total.

Now let us expand the above example and add another table right next to it.

	A	B	C	D	E	F	G	H
1		**Region**	**Target**	**Branch**		**Region**	**Target**	**Branch**
2		USA	New York	01234		Europe	Amsterdam	63845
3		USA	New York	12341		Europe	Amsterdam	71134
4		USA	New York	23544		Europe	Amsterdam	05730
5		USA	New York	73568		Europe	Amsterdam	48593
6		Asia	Shanghai	94678		Russia	Moscow	16344
7		Asia	Shanghai	25208		Russia	Moscow	64364
8		Asia	Shanghai	24621		Russia	Moscow	55435
9	Total			7				

You have two tables.

At this point, now matter what you do or how hard you try, you cannot make the macro function properly for the second table.

If you are wondering why, then this is the reason: you recorded it as an absolute macro.

Confused? Don't be.

Let us look at what this means by examining the code of the macro that we just created.

To do that, we now head back over to the Developer tab and then we select Macros. A dialog box will now open that shows all the macros that you have created. At this point, you should have just one macro and that would be the "AddTotal" or "TotalRecall" macro.

Go right ahead and select the macro that oy have created. Click on the Edit button. A new window will open up. This is your Visual Basic Editor window.

You might see a code that looks something like this.

Sub AddTotal()

Range("A9").Select

ActiveCell.FormulaR1C1 = "Total"

Range("D9").Select

ActiveCell.FormulaR1C1 = "=COUNTA(R[-7]C:R[-1]C)"

End Sub

Look closely at lines two and four of the code. What do you notice? Rather, what columns have you mentioned in the code? It shows A and D right?

When you gave Excel the command to simply choose the range of cells ending at A9 and D9, that is exactly what Excel did. When you select A9, then you get A9 and no other cell. Which is why it is difficult to simply replicate the result on another cell. It simply cannot happen.

Now what happens if we try to record the macro by using the relative reference option? Let us find out.

Mode Two: Recording with Relative References

When you use the option of Relative References, then Excel basically understands it as relative to the active cell you are working on.

This is why, you need to be more careful with your cell choice, both when you are recording the relative reference and when you are done recording to run the macro.

The first thing we are going to do is set up the table. Ideally, we are going to use the same table we used for the Absolute Reference example.

If you have not already, then here is the table for your use.

	A	B	C	D	E	F	G	H
1		**Region**	**Target**	**Branch**		**Region**	**Target**	**Branch**
2		USA	New York	01234		Europe	Amsterdam	63845
3		USA	New York	12341		Europe	Amsterdam	71134
4		USA	New York	23544		Europe	Amsterdam	05730
5		USA	New York	73568		Europe	Amsterdam	48593
6		Asia	Shanghai	94678		Russia	Moscow	16344
7		Asia	Shanghai	25208		Russia	Moscow	64364
8		Asia	Shanghai	24621		Russia	Moscow	55435
9								

Once the table has been set up, follow the below steps to work on it.

1. Head over toe the Developer tab and then select the Use Relative References option.

2. Before you begin the recording, make sure that you have selected the A1 cell.

3. Back to the Developer tab. Choose the Record Macro option.

4. Now we have to name to the macro. For the purpose of this example, we can use the name "AddRelative". However, you can use a name that you would like.

5. Next, you have to select This Workbook option as the save location.

6. Once you have done so, click on OK to begin your location.

7. Just like with the example with Absolute Reference, select the cell A9 and type in Total.

8. Now we are going to go to cell D9 and type in the following command: =COUNTA(D2:D8)

9. Head over to the Developer tab and then select the Stop Recording option. This will end the recording of Absolute Reference mode.

Once you have completed the recording, we are going to examine the code and find out just what happened.

To do that, we once again head back to the Developer tab and then select Macros. You will notice a list of macros here. If you have been following the tutorial strictly, then you should be able to notice two different macros. One should be for the Absolute Reference macro while the other should be for the Relative Reference. You should select the macro for the Relative Reference (which is named "AddRelative" in this case).

Click the Edit button to see a block of code that should look like this.

Sub AddRelative()

ActiveCell.Offset(9, 0).Range("A1").Select

ActiveCell.FormulaR1C1 = "Total"

ActiveCell.Offset(0, 3).Range("A1").Select

ActiveCell.FormulaR1C1 = "=COUNTA(R[-7]C:R[-1]C)"

End Sub

When you look the code, the changes will be rather obvious. At this point, you cannot see a specific cell being mentioned in the code at all.

Rather, if you look at line 2, then you will notice that the code features a unique property that appears in the form of an OFFSET command. When Excel reads this command, it basically does not fix on a particular cell.

What does OFFSET command actually mean and what does it tell Excel to do for you?

Offset is basically the property of Excel to shift to a specific number of cells from the starting cell, either in a vertical position (along columns) or in a horizontal position (along rows). This means that the command tells Excel to move a particular number of spots.

Let us look at the example above and use the explanation to find out what is happening.

In the code for Relative Reference, Excel is move 9 cells in the row. It will move 0 columns sideways. Basically, Excel is going to remain in the A1 column and move downwards.

Time to see the macro being played.

In order to do this, we are going to follow similar steps as the ones followed for Absolute Reference.

1. Click on cell A1

2. Go to the Developer tab and then select Macros.

3. You should now look for the "AddRelative" macro or whatever name you have given to the Relative Reference macro.

4. Click Run

5. Now, go over to cell F1

6. We are going to repeat the steps above so go the Developer Tab and select Macros

7. Select the "AddRelative" macro or the name that you have given to this macro.

8. Click on the Run button

You will notice that the macro not only runs on the first table, but also the second table created in the Excel sheet. This is because, unlike Absolute Reference, you are not entering a command that specifies a particular cell number. This means that the macro does not attach itself to certain cells. You are only telling the macro to work in relation to the cells that it has and the command it has been given.

Think of the above concept this way. You have given a map to a person. You have told the person to head straight and then take a left using a certain streets and those streets only. That is Absolute Reference.

You are now telling the person to head straight and then take a left, but you are giving the person general directions without forcing him or her to follow a particular street. That is Relative Reference.

The one thing that you have to make sure is that when you are working with Relative Reference, you have to select the right cell before you run the program.

Additionally, you have to ensure that the section of data that you want to focus on has the same number of rows and columns as the original section.

In the above example, columns A to D were the original sections. They had eight rows of data (one row for titles and the remaining seven rows for data). The next sections that we had focused on were columns E to H, which also had the same number of rows.

This is how macro recording works with both Absolute Reference and Relative Reference.

Here are a few points to remember when working with Excel macros.

1. Starting with Excel 2007, you now have the option to save worksheets that contains macros with a new file name. When you are using Excel 2010 for example, then you typically save the file using the .xlsx extension. When you save the file in that extension, you cannot save the macros as well. What happens to the macros? Excel removes all macros from the sheet if the sheet is saved using .xlsx extension. Which is why, you are now giving an option to save the sheet as an Excel Macro-Enabled Workbook. When you do this, the sheet gets a different extension, the .xlsm extension. The main reason for doing this is so that .xlsx does not contain any coding and hence is safe to open. However, a .xlsm file may contain coding that could harm your computer. The distinction in file extensions are made so that you can decide if you trust the source of the document to open it.

2. Another feature that you might notice with Excel 2010 (and future versions) is the upgrade in the Office security. One of the components of the Office security is the concept of trusted documents. What this means is that you are confident about the document to run macros in it. When you open a sheet that contains macros in it, then you might notice a message that pops up within a ribbon on top of the sheet that says that macros has been disabled. The way to enable the macros is by pressing the Enable button. Once you do that, the sheet remembers the action and the next time you open the sheet, you won't have to click on the Enable button again. Essentially, what you have done is give the command to the sheet that you trust the content and the macros within it.

When you are working with clients or with your colleagues, then this feature becomes important for two reasons:

a. You get to decide if you trust the source of the content.

b. You only have to Enable the macros once. This means that all the people working on the sheet are not annoyed by the constant message that the macros are disabled that pops up each time the sheet is open.

3. Sometimes, when you create macros, then you might want to have an easy way to run them. Fortunately, Excel has a solution for that. What you can do is assign a macro button to help you create a user interface called form controls to work with your macros. Sounds convenient? Then let us look at how you can activate this button. There are numerous types of form controls. You can choose to use buttons (which are commonly used as the controls) or you can choose to add scrollbars. Let us go back to the example we had used before and try to add a button to the macro. Here is how it is done:

a. Head over to the Developer tab and then choose the Insert button.

b. In the drop-down list that appears, click on the button Form Control option.

c. Click on the location where you would like to place the button. When you place the button control into your sheet, a special box called the Assign Macros dialog box appears on the sheet. You can then assign a macro to that button.

d. At this point, we have two macros – "AddTotal" and "AddRelative" – in the list of macros. Choose any one of them and assign them.

e. You are now ready to use the buttons!

CHAPTER 12

Executing A Macro Upon Modification Of Some Cells In Excel

You already know that by now that MS Excel can be used for developing macros, which are only accessible when a value is entered in a particular cell of a worksheet or sheet, which is open at that moment. Be aware that calling macros for no reason will only slow the speed of your sheet and lower its performance.

In several instances, the macro executes only when there is an entered value in the sheet cells. You need to make sure whether the ActiveCell is such an element. For that, you will need to use the Intersect method on the cell range and the ActiveCell for verification of the currently active cell as being part of the specified range. If the ActiveCell is present within the range, and has the key cells present in it, then the macro will be called. For this, the VB macro will be created in the following way:

1. First, you will right click in the Project window on the tab for Sheet1, and after that click on the ViewCode option. Upon doing so, you will see the Module sheet open behind the tab for Sheet1.

2. You will then have to type the following code in the VBE.

Private Sub Worksheet_Change(ByVal Target As Range)

Dim KeyCells As Range

'KeyCells is the variable that consists of cells, which will send a notification upon altering a value in them.

Set KeyCells Range("A1:C10")

*If Not Application.Intersect(KeyCells, Range(Target.Address))_*

Is Nothing Then

'This displays a message upon changing one of the specific cells.

MsgBox "Cell" & Target.Adress & "has been altered."

End If

End Sub

3. After that, you have to click on the option saying close and return to MS Excel that you can find in the File tab menu.

Handling and Trapping Macro Errors

You will need to add the program lines in all the macros for processing and intercepting any error when they occur in the code. You can frequently witness errors occurring in the macro when it is executing. This can be due to several reasons, like typos in the code and execution of a macro in scenarios that it was not programmed to run in the first place.

If you add an error trapping function to your macro, you will know the output due to an error. You will have the power to regulate the error occurring in the code. Thus, you have the authority to take the necessary steps to handle it without being confused about what could be wrong with your code.

If you fail to include an error handling function in your code, then it could lead to an irrelevant behavior by your Excel. The worst that can happen due to this mess is that the other users may not be able to see the latest changes in your worksheets. Plus, Excel might also freeze in such a case and there can be loss of data due to it. Plus, all these issues can even occur at once, leading to a more cumbersome situation.

Note that you want other users to not leave their own reaction to various error messages that may occur in your work. For instance,

A Run-time error '513' may return that can cause an error message saying:

"Application-defined or object-defined error"

Thus, you are going to need the help of error handling functions to execute the necessary steps beforehand, and without any other user's involvement.

Basic Error Handling Function

You can find several ways to add a code for error handling actions in your macro. You can study the following code, which is one such example.

Sub MacroName()

On Error GoTo errHandler

Macro code

ProcDone:

Exit Sub

errHandler:

MsgBox Err.Number & ":" & Err.Description

Resume procDone

End Sub

With the on Error line of code present in the above VBA program, you are turning on the error trapping function. This code will offer a tracking system for all the errors that may occur in a macro. The error will be returned in the VBA object known as Err. If an error occurs in the code, the statement: "On Error Goto errHandler," Excel will instruct the macro to stop running the operation. It will then move to the errHandler statement from where it will continue with the necessary operations.

With the MSGBox statement, a message will be displayed on the screen that provides with information related to the error occurred. Err.Number is the identification number provided for the particular error object, which is taken from the library for VBA errors. Furthermore, the Err.Description statement decribes the error. With procDone, the macro will continue running the statement label procDone.

Refined Codes For Error Handling

Let's make an assumption that you have added the code for error handling in your macro discussed in the previous section. Upon evaluating the macro, an error takes place. So, you get a message displayed that lets you known the nature and number of the occurred error. You will have to carry a revision with the error handler in response to the particular error faced. In the example provided, the error that occurs is 1234.

```
Sub MacroName()


On Error Goto errHandler

Macro code

procDone:

Exit Sub

errHandler:

Select Case Err.Number

Case 1234

Error handling code for error 1234

Case Else

'Every error outstanding

MsgBox Err.Number & ":" & Err.Description

End Select

Resume procDone

End Sub
```

Upon testing the macro to check for other errors that may be possible in the code, you may want to extend the functionality of the Select case command along with other suitable cases for this code. The following code will offer you a refined messages for your macro:

```
Sub MacroName()

On Error Goto errHandler

Dim msg$, title$, icon&

Macro code

procDone:

Exit Sub

errHandler:

icon& = vbOKOnly +vbCritical

Select Case Err.Number

Case 53

title$ = "File Missing"

msg$ = "Macro unable to find the necessary file."

msg$ = msg$  vbNewline & vbNewLine

msg$ = msg$ & "Please inform this to the developer."

Case Else

Title$ = "Error not anticipated"

msg$ = Err.Number  ":" & Err.Description

msg$ = msg$ & vbNewline  vbNewLine

msg$ = msg$ & "Please note down this message"
```

End Select

MsgBox Err.Number & ":" & Err.Description

Resume procDone

End Sub

Macro Debugging

The Debug Button and the Error Message Notification

While you are executing a macro, you will occasionally run into an error message that says: "Run-time Error," followed by an error message. You can find three types of buttons available on the box for the error message. These are: Debug, Help, and End.

You can stop the macro when facing error with the End button present on the error box. If you want to access more information about the error, then you can press the Help button. Pressing the Help button will take you to a MS site that has a list of possible reasons behind the error that has occurred. You will also have the relevant solutions for each of the errors specified there. For solving the issue, you can choose the Debug button, which then takes you to the Visual basic editor.

Conclusion

People have a misconception about macros; they think that to get started, you might need the knowledge of advanced coding. Here is the reality; while coding is an integral part of macros, it does not mean that you will be spending endless hours trying to go through the basics of coding and then trying to master its complex forms.

One of the things that makes macros convenient to work with is the fact that you – like anybody else – can pick up the fundamentals and then get started on it.

But apart from the above advice, let me share a few tips that you might find useful while you are working on Excel macros.

1. My recommendation would be to always begin from the home position. This makes it easier to you to plot your data and create macros for them. It help you create additional tables as compared to the first one or in relation to it. In order to start from the home position, all you have to do is hit CTRL + Home.

2. If you would like to navigate, make sure you are using the directional keys. Once you start begin working on macros, you are going to have a lot of data to look through. Scrolling would mean that you are going to skip data that you require. Your navigation should be fixed to Up, Down, Left, Right, and the End keys.

3. This is an important tip and it is one even professionals with years of experience tend to commit. Create small macros that cater to specific function. Let us understand this tip with the help of an example. If you would like to sort through the data, then create a macro for it. If you then decide to take information from the data, then create a separate macro for it. Do not combine all your macros for two vital reasons:

   a. If you combine various tasks into one macro, then your macro ends up running slower. The more you add into a macro, the slower it runs. Initially, this might not be a problem but when you begin to add more formations and complex information, then you are really going to feel the slow pace of the process.

   b. Secondly, we are all capable of making mistakes. This means that often, a macro might end up having an error and won't run properly. In such situations, you should be able to figure out which task of a macro is causing the problem and fix it. The task of identifying a problem becomes difficult if you group different tasks into one macro. You might end up looking through each and every line of code to find out where the problem lies. If you have a small macro, this might not be a problem. But if you end up having many lines of code, then you are going to spend a lot of time trying to find out the problem.

4. When you have fixed information or fixed data, make sure you enter it in advance before you start working on variable data. Let us assume that you have a column called "City". You are working on only one city, which is "New York". In that case, make sure you fill up the column with New York before beginning on any macro. That way, you save the

precious time filling up each and every cell with the same entry and second, you won't have to run macro each time you create the same entry. Macros are effective when they are used for complex tasks and working with different sets of data. It becomes pointless when you are merely using it for the same data repeatedly.

5. Take advantage of keyboard shortcuts. It might be a little cumbersome working with the shortcuts when you start, but once you get the hang of it, you won't have any problems with the shortcuts at all. For example, if you would like to highlight a specific column, then all you have to do is hold down the END key, and the hit SHIFT + DOWN key. The entire column will be highlighted for you without changing anything within the macro.

6. Remember that if you do not enter the keystrokes as recommended by Excel, then your macro is bound to fail. This is why, you have to make sure that you get your keystrokes right. Take the time to learn some of the shortcuts and key combinations before working on your macro.

7. If you would like to know the shortcuts to the menus, then all you have to do is hit the ALT key while inside the sheet. This will display the menu shortcuts. Once you have made note of the shortcuts, hit the ALT key again and then the shortcut highlights will disappear.

8. If you would like to separate names within a sheet from one column into two, then there is an easy way to go about it. The first thing you have to do is CTRL + HOME and then press CTRL + A. Once that is done, head over to Data and the select Text to Columns. In the first dialog box that appears, click on the Delimited and then click on Next. In the next window that opens up, you have to choose the character that

delimits your text. We know that the common character between the first and last name is Space. So check on the option that says Space and then click Next. Finally, in the last box, choose the option Text and hit Finish. Once you perform the above actions, your names will be split into two columns.

With that, I hope you are ready to begin your macros journey. Enjoy the process and hope macros brings a world of convenience to your Excel workings.

References

Add your personal Excel Macros to the ribbon. (2019). Retrieved from https://www.get-digital-help.com/2013/12/03/add-your-personal-excel-macros-to-the-ribbon/

Chandran, M. (2019). How to run macro based on cell value in Excel?. Retrieved from https://www.extendoffice.com/documents/excel/4420-excel-run-macro-based-on-cell-value.html

Create a button for a macro - HowTo-Outlook. (2019). Retrieved from https://www.howto-outlook.com/howto/macrobutton.htm

How to Build a Custom Excel Toolbar of VBA Macros. (2019). Retrieved from https://www.makeuseof.com/tag/custom-excel-toolbar-vba-macros/

How to Call or Run a Another Macro From a Macro - Excel Campus. (2019). Retrieved from https://www.excelcampus.com/library/vba-call-statement-run-macro-from-macro/

How to Optimize VBA Performance. (2019). Retrieved from https://www.spreadsheet1.com/how-to-optimize-vba-performance.html

Optimize Slow VBA Code. Speed Up Efficient VBA Code/Macros. (2019). Retrieved from https://www.ozgrid.com/VBA/SpeedingUpVBACode.htm

Shepherd, R. (2004). Excel VBA macro programming. New York: McGraw-Hill/Osborne.

Troy, A., & Gonzalez, J. (2006). Office VBA macros you can use today. Uniontown: Holy Macro! Books.

Walkenbach ... (2013). Excel 2003 Power Programming with VBA. Hoboken: Wiley.

Walkenbach, J. (2004). Excel VBA Programming For Dummies. John Wiley & Sons.